MAGNET® INVESTING

MAGNET® INVESTING

build a portfolio and pick winning stocks
using your home computer
(2nd Edition)

Jordan L. Kimmel

With an introduction by John Downes
Co-author of *Beating the Dow*

Including a Mathematical Backtest by T. Owen Carroll, Ph.D.

Published by:
Next Decade, Inc.
39 Old Farmstead Road
Chester, New Jersey 07930-2732 USA
908-879-6625

Library of Congress Cataloging in Publication Data

Kimmel, Jordan L.
    Magnet investing : build a portfolio and pick winning stocks using your home computer
    / Jordan L. Kimmel ; with an introduction by John Downes.--[2nd ed.]
       p. cm.
    "Including a mathematical backtest by T. Owen Carroll, Ph.D."
    Includes index.
    ISBN: 0-9626003-8-5 (pbk.)
     1. Investment analysis--Data processing. 2. Portfolio management--Data processing. 3.
    Microcomputers. I. Carroll, T. Owen. II. Title.

    HG4529 .K563 2000
    332.63'2'0285416--dc21

                                       00-033943

Printed and bound by Data Reproductions Corporation, Auburn Hills, Michigan

> This publication is designed to provide accurate and authoritative information in regard to the subject matter covered. It is sold with the understanding that the publisher is not engaged in rendering legal, accounting, or other professional service. If legal advice or other expert assistance is required, the services of a competent professional person should be sought.
>
> *—From the declaration of principles jointly adopted by a committee of the American Bar Association and a committee of publishers.*

To my wife and children

Contents

Appendices

List of Charts

List of Tables

About The Author and Contributor

JORDAN L. KIMMEL

Jordan Kimmel, a leading stock expert and private money manager, has been the President of Magnet Management, LLC since 1997. As such, he directs the application of the MAGNET® Stock Selection Process in a variety of disciplines: Hedge funds, mutual funds, unit trusts, and retail brokerage. Mr. Kimmel's stock picking methodology and accurate predictions of recent swings in the stock market have earned him multiple appearances on national television and radio shows, including CNBC, CNN and Bloomberg. He is also quoted extensively in newspapers and radio across the nation.

Mr. Kimmel also serves as First Montauk Securities Corp.'s Market Strategist. As such, he uses his MAGNET® Stock Selection Process to manage the firm's Focus List. In addition, Mr. Kimmel manages a retail brokerage office (Magnet Investment Group) for First Montauk Securities Corp., one of the nation's largest independent securities brokerage firms. The Magnet Investment Group offers full brokerage services, heavily emphasizing individual stocks, bonds and mutual funds.

Prior to inception of his company in April 1997, Mr. Kimmel served as a First Vice President at Dean Witter. Earlier in his career he was a First

Vice President at Paine Webber and A.G. Edwards. His experience also includes five years with the New York City Mayor's Office, where he was responsible for financial analysis and planning. A graduate of the State University of New York at Stony Brook, Mr. Kimmel holds a B.A. in Economics and an M.S. in Urban Policy Sciences. The Manhattan native is also a graduate of the prestigious Bronx High School of Science.

The Magnet Investment Group is located at Millbrook Plaza, 1201 Sussex Turnpike, Randolph, NJ 07869. You can reach him on the worldwide web at www.magnetinvesting.com

T. Owen Carroll

Dr. Carroll is a professor of Finance in the W. Averell Harriman School of Management at the State University of New York at Stony Brook. He received a B.S. in Engineering Physics from the University of California at Berkeley and a Ph.D. in Applied Physics and Electrical Engineering from Cornell University. Dr. Carroll was awarded the Distinguished Teaching Award in the College of Engineering at Stony Brook, the Chancellor's Award for Excellence in Teaching from the State University of New York, and was one of the founding professors of the W. Averell Harriman School of Management. He has served as a consultant to the governments of Canada and Thailand, as well as CITIBANK, Nabisco, PPG and other corporations.

Dr. Carroll is currently engaged in research and teaching in Computational Finance, the applications of dynamic systems techniques to financial time series and related areas of financial research. He also has been a Director of Research and consultant in money management firms engaged in aggressive, high turnover portfolio management and computerized trade implementation.

Preface

The twelve-month period that has elapsed since the release of the first edition of *Magnet® Investing* has been an exciting time for the Magnet Investment Group. The book's model portfolio achieved returns of over 90%, and we have received tremendous professional feedback. Wall Street has acknowledged and accepted the MAGNET® Stock Selection Process, because of its superior returns across all indexes. Our disciplined approached has been adopted by a major mutual fund and a separate unit investment trust group, and I continue to be invited back for television and radio appearances on most major financial news shows including CNBC, CNN and Bloomberg.

I had no doubt when I developed the MAGNET® process that our common sense approach of combining value, growth, and momentum investing, using a revenue based model, would generate a great deal of interest. I look forward to sharing our proven MAGNET® process with you.

This book is the result of the combined efforts of many. I have spent the last twenty years as in the professional investment field as a fund manager, stockbroker and investor. I have read about countless methodologies and sought out many so-called "experts." My experience has taught invaluable lessons that enabled me to develop the MAGNET® system of stock selection.

During the development of the system, I turned to Dr. T. Owen Carroll a Professor of Business at the W. Averell Harriman School of Management at the State University of New York at Stony Brook (my alma mater). Dr. Carroll is renowned for his insightful research within the financial community, and for the past few years, he has been rigorously and meticulously backtesting the MAGNET® Stock Selection Process, both independently and in combination with several professional groups that test new methodologies. The results are powerful. The process that I have developed has produced a ten-year average annualized return of over 30%.

The combined efforts of Dr. Carroll, and my staff have led to what may be the most effective system to uncover winning stocks. We were also fortunate to have spent countless hours with John Downes, the best selling co-author of *Beating the Dow*. John's insight and curiosity led us to ask ourselves many questions as our backtesting process continued.

In addition to introducing the MAGNET® Stock Selection Process, the goal of this book is to help investors improve their returns. I will attempt to illustrate that to the extent an individual can:

1.   Develop a personalized long-term plan;

2.   Receive timely and accurate information;

3.   Utilize a disciplined stock selection process and;

4.   Utilize unemotional portfolio and money management skills, he can significantly increase his investment success.

I have always been interested in investing. I grew up in a middle class family as the youngest of four children. My parents owned and operated a small retail store, and during my childhood, tried their hands in a number of ventures. Business was discussed regularly over dinner and the concept of "profit" was an early lesson to me. At the age of eight, I bought thirty-five shares of stock in H.J. Heinz Co. (the ketchup people). I cannot recall how I saved up the money or how I placed the order, but I remember checking the price in the newspaper regularly. I was probably the company's proudest shareholder.

I later enrolled at The Bronx High School of Science. By this time, I was buying options on the stock market, and I developed a reputation as someone not to bet against. I continued my education and earned a Bachelor's degree in Economics and a Master's degree in Urban Policy Sciences at the State University of New York at Stony Brook, with heavy emphasis on statistics and quantitative analysis. This has proven to be very beneficial throughout my investment career. In addition, paying my own way through college gave me an early understanding of the value of both money and education. The education was good, but nowhere as enlightening as my "hands on" experiences in the stock market.

For several years after graduation, I worked in a variety of financial positions for the City of New York, and then found my way to Wall Street. Over the last dozen years, I have worked as a financial advisor at some of the country's leading brokerage firms. I have learned professional lessons too vast to enumerate. This experience has been supplemented by reading almost every investment book that has been published in the past hundred years. I am now forty-one years old with over thirty years of investment experience.

Despite my early interest in money, the desire to accumulate wealth is not my only focus. I have always believed in a balanced approach to life. Have fun, enjoy your family, experience life, and invest well.

For the sake of easy reading, I refer to all investors as "he". This is not intended to insult my female readers, nor my wife.

To take full advantage of the MAGNET® system you must have a computer program that enables you to access the powerful search programs that are available. Several companies provide investors with a computerized stock monitoring and evaluation program, among other investment services. They include Telescan, Telechart 2000, Zacks Investment Research, Quicken, Market Guide, Hoovers and Yahoo. Most of these programs combine all of the essential fundamental and technical indicators.

The order of the subject matter in this book is presented as a series of stepping-stones. The first several chapters will teach the reader how to develop a winning approach to investing. They include the evolution of a stock investor, and discuss the merits of proper planning, dedication to learning, and the investor's attitude. The next chapters cover bonds, asset allocation, timing, the "buy and hold" strategy, profitable portfolio management, and how to maximize your home computer. Throughout these chapters the reader will find many interesting charts that enhance the discussion. Some of them have been pulled from old files and may look a bit fuzzy. Finally, in Chapter 14, I introduce the MAGNET® Stock Selection Process, and the next two chapters will show why the system works and how to use it. I will also discuss the returns from the model portfolios from the first edition and explain why certain stocks outperformed others. I will also address why the "complex" search outperformed the "simple." We then perform a new search and discuss tax efficiency. Chapter 20 will provide you with my updated "recommended reading list" of excellent books about various facets of investing. Finally, I conclude with a chapter called "Putting it All Together".

At the end of the book are several appendices including a mathematical presentation and backtesting of the MAGNET® system, the results of the Prosearches performed in Chapter 18, samples of former MAGNET® stocks, a list of potential MAGNET® investments, and a glossary of investment terms.

In summary, the Magnet chapters contain a unique, successful and actionable approach to improving the process of selecting stocks. The rest of the book was written and included because there is a lack of quality material available to serve as a primer in teaching the millions of people still mystified by Wall Street.

This book is about building and managing a successful stock portfolio by combining the resources of a powerful new stock selection process and your computer.

Jordan Kimmel

Acknowledgments

Bringing this book to completion took a great effort and more time than I expected. What started out as a simple primer on investments with an introduction of the MAGNET® Stock Selection Process turned into much more.

I owe thanks to Dr. T. Owen Carroll for his tireless work in the backtesting process of the MAGNET® system itself. The time, effort, and insight of Dr. Carroll have helped me to develop this selection process that I, in turn, hope will help many in the future.

I would like to give special thanks to Ned Davis Research, Inc. for the use of their great work and illustrative charts. It is no wonder why they lead the way in institutional research for Wall Street.

I would like to thank Michael Carty from New Millenium for his keen insights into Magnet, and the assistance he provided in editing the second edition.

I am also grateful to the many other professionals that took the time to review the book and provide insightful help along the way.

I would like to thank Telescan™ for its assistance over the years in helping me become a better investor by providing an ever-improving package to work with.

I am grateful to John Downes for his months of collaboration and effort in the early stages of the book. His curiosity and probing helped us along the way.

I would like to thank the dozens of excellent Lafayette College students who over the last several years have worked endless hours on our spreadsheets, while we push towards perfection. Your efforts have contributed greatly.

I would like to give an extra big thanks to my right hand at the Magnet

Investment Group, Tom Doyle, for coordinating and following through on so much that was required throughout the process.

Lastly, and most importantly, I give my credit, thanks, and appreciation to my wife Barbara who really made this book happen again. With this edition, Barbara took a book that we were both proud of, and found dozens of ways to improve it.

I hope that the second edition helps many more investors. The positive feedback from investors who read the first book gave us the inspiration to publish a second edition.

Disclaimer

The purpose of this book is to provide interested individuals with a basic understanding of the complexities of investing and to introduce the MAG-NET® Stock Selection Process. It is presented with the understanding that the publisher and author are not engaged in rendering personal investment advice or other professional services in this book, only in sharing information in regard to the subject matter covered. If investment or other expert assistance is required, the services of a competent professional should be sought.

This manual was not written to provide all the information that is available to the author/and or publisher, but to complement, amplify and supplement other texts and available information. While every effort has been made to ensure that this book is as complete and accurate as possible, there may be mistakes, either typographical or in content. Therefore, this text should be used as a general guide only, and not as the ultimate source of investment information. Furthermore, this book contains current information only up to the printing date. Past performance is no guarantee of future results.

Information herein was obtained from various sources whose accuracy is not guaranteed. Neither the information, nor any opinion expressed constitutes an offer to buy or sell any securities. Opinions expressed and information are subject to change without notice.

The author and Next Decade, Inc. shall not be held liable, nor be responsible to any person or entity with respect to any loss or damage caused, or alleged to be caused, directly or indirectly by the information contained in this book.

If you do not wish to be bound by the above, you may return this book to the publisher for a full refund.

Introduction

by John Downes

Co-Author of *Beating the Dow*

In 1990, I met a baby-boomer named Mike O'Higgins and with him wrote *Beating the Dow*. That book, which became a best seller, introduced a market-beating stock strategy of Mike's creation that was so simple it caused a revolution in personal investing.

The system—you know it as The Dogs of the Dow or the Dow Dividend Strategy—operates on the premise that the thirty stocks in the select Dow Jones Industrial averages are more resilient than risky and it works like this. The Dow stocks, household names like General Electric and Exxon, being run by human beings, have problems from time to time. The market reacts (actually it overreacts, typically) by driving their prices down and their yields up (yield is the annual dividend as a percentage of the market price). That's when you buy. When the same companies, having huge financial resources and being under intense shareholder pressure, fix their problems, typically in a year or two, the market drives their prices up and their yields down. That's when you sell.

Portfolios based on this "no-brainer," structured using ten minutes each year and then left alone until the following year, have averaged over 21% for 25 years, have stayed above water in the worst bear markets, and have outperformed 80% of all mutual funds. The attraction, again, was simplicity. In fact, the first chapter in the book was titled "Keep It Simple." The very last sentence in the book is "In investing, simplicity beats complexity." Simplicity appeals to me.

In 1997 I met another baby-boomer named Jordan Kimmel, who also wanted to talk about doing a book. He showed me a stock-picking system he devised and calls MAGNET®, that is the very antithesis of simplicity. It uses practically every tool of fundamental and technical analysis that exists. It focuses on a universe of some 10,000 stocks that represent every industry and niche-industry. The companies it selects run the gamut of big and small, old and new, income- and growth. MAGNET® embraces complexity the way *Beating the Dow* embraced simplicity.

Ironically, though, MAGNET® appealed to my simple mind the same way Beating the Dow did and it had some extra attractions in terms of potential total returns and containment of risk. Investment software available in the 1990's has made it possible to reduce complexity to simplicity. To use a baseball analogy, it's like the switch that lights up the ballpark for a night-game; there's a lot of intricate wiring involved, but if we know which switches are which, we can play ball.

A number of user-friendly computer programs—Jordan uses Telescan—store voluminous data on thousands of stocks and analyze that data any way you ask them to. Depending on how skillfully the resources are used, stocks can be identified that produce spectacular returns with quantifiably lower risk.

The genius, which in this case is Jordan Kimmel's, is in knowing what questions to ask. Jordan, who has the performance numbers to prove it, is in a class by himself in terms of the amount of reading and research he has done, his hands-on experience as a money manager, and his exceptional intelligence and investment judgment. But you don't have to be Jordan to use the system he has devised.

MAGNET® enables an average personal investor to find, among thousands of stocks, the rare few combining attributes that in traditional (pre-computer) analysis have been considered incompatible—momentum and value, for example. When found together, and in combination with other fundamental characteristics establishing financial strength and earnings potential, such attributes can be doubly powerful.

But MAGNET® looks also at institutional ownership, insider holdings, executive compensation and equity participation, and at qualitative factors involving management and product development. Finally, MAGNET® uses state-of-the-art technical analysis techniques to determine the most opportune times to buy and sell.

In today's institution-dominated market, the individual investor has flexibility in buying and selling stocks that muscle-bound institutions lack. Access to information about companies and the ability to analyze that information, advantages traditionally enjoyed by institutional investors, is now available to you and me through computer databases and easy-to-use computer programs.

The opportunities for individual investors to outperform professional money managers have never been greater. The computer has revolutionized the art and science of stock picking. Jordan Kimmel's MAGNET® method may be the first state-of-the-art system simple enough to enable average investors to beat the pros.

John Downes

1

Preview

"The man who masters himself masters the universe."
Robert Krausz

"Nothing in life is to be feared. It is only to be understood."
Marie Curie

I would like to spend a moment addressing current stock market conditions. As most of you are aware the "raging bull" has been charging through the major averages for many years. Both the length of this bull market and the size of its gains have surprised most market participants.

Unfortunately, two groups of individuals have been left behind in the bull's dust: Those simply unwilling or unable to invest, and those that owned the "wrong" stocks. This is because the last several years of this bull market have been primarily a large capitalization stock phenomenon. Most smaller stocks, as measured by an unweighted advance-decline line, have been in a decline for years. The charts at the end of this chapter tell a story not captured by the public or the media. The bull market of the 1990's left many investors with disappointing returns. Stock selection is critical.

We go to print in mid-Summer 2000, at a strikingly similar time to our first edition. We have experienced a sharp and sudden selloff in the markets. The swift and devastating bear has caused the average Over the Counter stock to decline more than 50% off its high. At today's lofty valuation levels, stock selection has been, and will continue to be, even more important than usual. What is so exciting is that a burst of confidence and money flow has created a new uptrend being lead by a few "old names" along with many "new MAGNET®" stocks.

The stock market is currently at levels previously unseen when measured by historical indicators such as price to earnings ratios (P/E), dividend yields, and price to book. Amid what appears to be wild speculation among technology stocks, there is a large and smart group of financial analysts talking of an impending crash.

I remain a long-term bull on our stock market. New companies are always emerging that will represent the dominant businesses and industries of the future. The stock market will continue to function as a vehicle to generate financial success to those that have the tools to identify these great companies.

The lessons of the market over the past fifteen years helped me to develop and refine a system that identifies a pool of potentially great stocks. Chart a course to find them. I have included worksheets in Chapter 5 to help keep you on your path.

Finally, I realize that many individuals simply do not have the time to effectively manage a portfolio, nor to implement the MAGNET® Stock Selection Process. Feel free to call on the resources of my "think tank." We have assembled a powerful group of individuals that are using the MAGNET® Stock Selection Process to help those interested in achieving strong investment results.

CHART 1-1

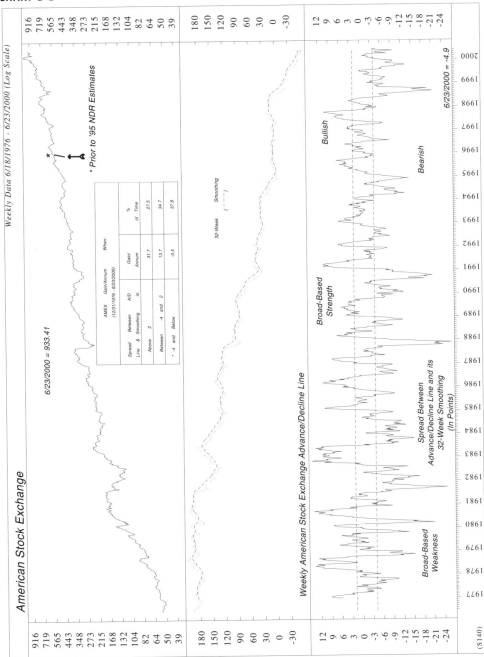

Courtesy of Ned Davis Research

Simply stated, the advance-decline line represents the difference between advancing issues and declining issues each day (or week depending on the calculation). Stocks that remain unchanged for the day are not included. The American Stock Exchange Index and the weekly advance-decline line give the appearance of two very different markets. An investor needed to be very selective in this bull market. Stock selection counts.

CHART 1-2

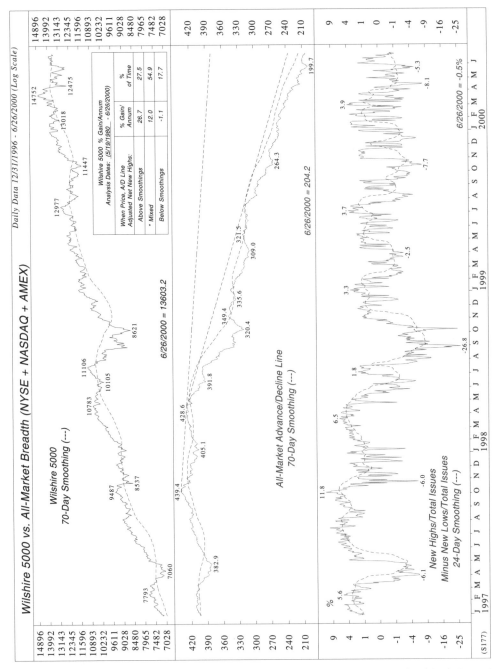

Courtesy of Ned Davis Research

Take a close look at the advance-decline lines. Since 1995, they have told a totally different story from what the averages, or indexes, were showing.

CHART 1-3

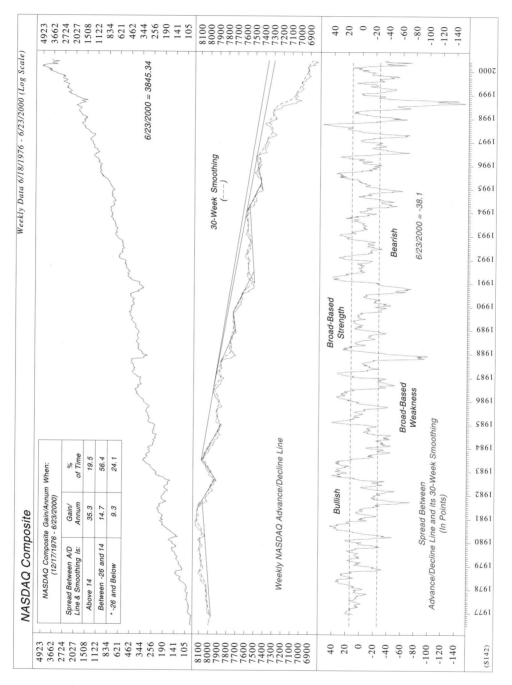

Courtesy of Ned Davis Research

The broad Over the Counter Market was declining for years while the ultra large capitalization "favorites" painted a picture of a raging bull market. This chart shows that the weekly advance-decline line actually turned negative in 1980.

Accepting the Challenge of Investing

"No profession requires more hard work, intelligence, patience, and mental discipline than successful speculation."

Robert Rhea

Let's talk about some current (and common) realities that make financial freedom so difficult to obtain, including shifts in costs of living, life expectancy and inflation.

When asked about their primary financial concern, many individuals express the fear of outliving their assets– in other words, running out of money during old age. These are well-founded feelings for a number of reasons. People are living longer and the cost of living continues to spiral upward, despite reports of low inflation. As a result, major demographic changes have lead individuals away from savings accounts and into longer-term investments. In addition, the period following retirement is longer for most people because life expectancy has increased, and retirement often comes earlier. Finally, the costs of education, health care, and the possibility of caring for one's parents are requiring individuals to examine their investment plans in a new light.

Our grandparents' idea of sound fiscal planning was opening and maintaining a bank account that earned interest. This carried forward to our parents' generation, and even into our own. Many senior citizens now find themselves unable to maintain an acceptable lifestyle because they did not understand what their financial needs would be, as they grew older. The modern investor is beginning to see that a different approach needs to be taken.

If all our future financial needs were known, and the costs were fixed, the blueprint for investing would be easy. Unfortunately, we are surrounded by uncertainty. While we may have expectations of purchasing certain items in the future, we have no way of knowing what price we will be asked to pay at that time. This is because inflation keeps our annual costs rising. Therefore the goal of investing is to manage our discretionary income in a way that it outpaces the rate of inflation, thereby maintaining our purchasing power.

An investment career is launched the first day that an individual obtains discretionary money. A child begins to collect items with the money saved through gifts and allowance, and soon, material possessions like baseball cards or Barbie dolls become more desirable than hard currency in a savings account. A child is accumulating possessions and wealth, and is already making decisions between current consumption, and saving for future purchases.

Later in life the stakes increase, but the underlying process remains the same. How should each one of us allocate discretionary assets so that life is most like we wish it to be? Perhaps future security and long term planning for financial independence need to replace some current material desires.

Money that is allocated for the accumulation of financial assets can be invested in one of two ways:

1. Lending– you can lend your money to an institution with the condition that you will be paid a prearranged percentage on your principal. Examples of this style of investment are a Certificate of Deposit at a bank, or an institutional corporate bond.

2. Ownership– you can own a portion of a company whose stock is publicly traded i.e., invest in common stocks.

Understanding the obvious and subtle differences between stocks and bonds is essential, and is addressed in Chapter 8. Remember, if money is not wisely invested, the effects of inflation will erode purchasing power.

We need to examine our personal circumstances and plot a course towards financial freedom, considering the demographic shifts discussed in this chapter. This goal can become a reality by starting early, developing a plan that complements your personality, and sticking to it.

CHAPTER

3

Get Started Early

"It's important to start...start from right where you are."
Wally Amos, inventor of Famous Amos cookies

*"Selling a soybean contract short is worth
two years at the Harvard Business School."*
Robert Stovall

"Nothing is more sacred than compound returns."
Ben Franklin

To achieve financial freedom, it is critical to start investing at a young age. This is important for two reasons:

1. The longer your money is invested in the stock market, the greater the opportunity to create wealth. This is known as compounding returns.

2. Acquiring investment knowledge and expertise takes years.

The long-term results of compounding returns are truly outstanding. In fact, Mark Twain called it "one of the wonders of the world." Table 3-1 and Chart 3-1 compare investment returns being compounded tax-free to a similar investment that is subject to a 25% income tax rate. These highlight the importance in establishing tax-deferred accounts at an early age.

TTable 3-1. TABLE OF COMPOUNDED RETURNS

	At 12% Tax Free	At 12% With 25% Income Tax
Year 1	$ 100,000.00	$ 100,000.00
	$ 112,000.00	$ 109,000.00
	$ 125,440.00	$ 118,810.00
	$ 140,492.80	$ 129,502.90
	$ 157,351.94	$ 141,158.16
	$ 176,234.17	$ 153,862.40
	$ 197,382.27	$ 167,710.01
	$ 221,068.14	$ 182,803.91
	$ 247,596.32	$ 199,256.26
Year 10	$ 277,307.88	$ 217,189.33
	$ 310,584.82	$ 236,736.37
	$ 347,855.00	$ 258,042.64
	$ 389,597.60	$ 281,266.48
	$ 436,349.31	$ 306,580.46
	$ 488,711.23	$ 334,172.70
	$ 547,356.58	$ 364,248.25
	$ 613,039.37	$ 397,030.59
	$ 686,604.09	$ 432,763.34
	$ 768,996.58	$ 471,712.04
Year 20	$ 861,276.17	$ 514,166.13
	$ 964,629.31	$ 560,441.08
	$ 1,080,384.83	$ 610,880.77
	$ 1,210,031.01	$ 665,860.04
	$ 1,355,234.73	$ 725,787.45
	$ 1,517,862.89	$ 791,108.32
	$ 1,700,006.44	$ 862,308.07
	$ 1,904,007.21	$ 939,915.79

	$ 2,132,488.08	$1,024,508.21
	$ 2,388,386.65	$1,116,713.95
Year 30	$ 2,674,993.05	$1,217,218.21
	$ 2,995,992.21	$1,326,767.85
	$ 3,355,511.28	$1,446,176.95
	$ 3,758,172.63	$1,576,332.88
	$ 4,209,153.35	$1,718,202.84
	$ 4,714,251.75	$1,872,841.09
	$ 5,279,961.96	$2,041,396.79
	$ 5,913,557.39	$2,225,122.50
	$ 6,623,184.28	$2,425,383.53
	$ 7,417,966.39	$2,643,668.05
	$ 8,308,122.36	$2,881,598.17

The other advantage in starting early is that by leaving your assets invested in stocks, you increase your chances of making money over the long run. Following are four charts (Charts 3-2 to 3-5) that show one-year, five-year, ten-year, and twenty-year holding period returns per annum for stocks. This sequence of charts reveals that since December 31, 1926, the odds of profitable investing in any one year were 74.3%, further emphasizing that the longer an investor stays in the stock market, the greater the chance of generating a positive return.

Remember that an investor who is just starting out has a tremendous amount to learn, and will make many mistakes. It is the lessons learned from these mistakes that can help the savvy investor make real money as he broadens his knowledge base. "Evolving as an investor" requires the ability to "learn from your mistakes." These are important concepts and are covered in later chapters.

In summary, those who get started early have the advantage of compounding returns, and time to learn from their mistakes.

CHART 3-1

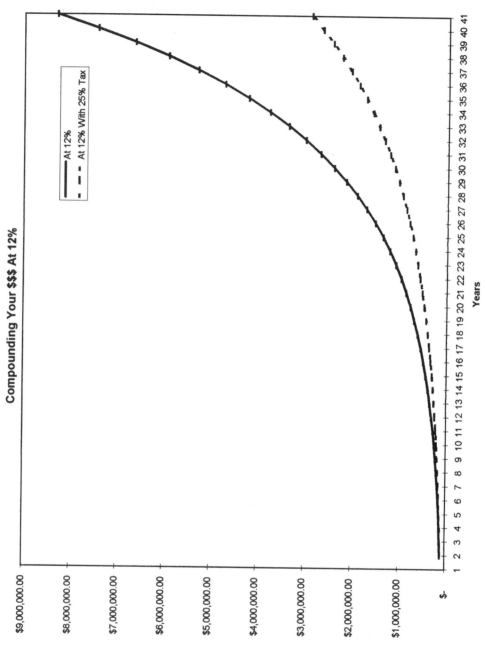

Courtesy of MAGNET® Management LLC

It is amazing how much appreciation occurs over time when money is compounded, even more so when it is in a tax-deferred account.

CHART 3-2

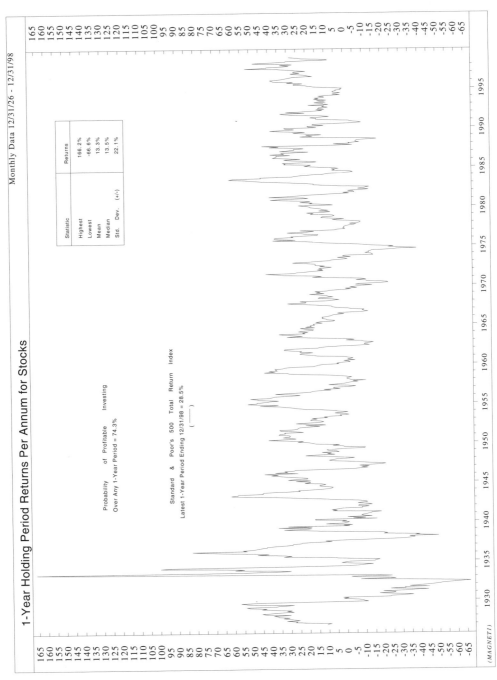

Courtesy of Ned Davis Research

Even though the odds of making money are high (74.3%), you can expect volatility in any given year.

CHART 3-3

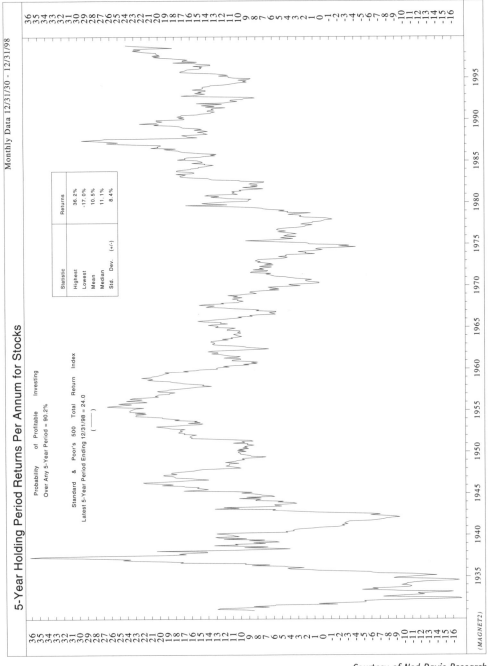

Statistic	Returns
Highest	36.2%
Lowest	-17.0%
Mean	10.5%
Median	11.1%
Std. Dev. (+/-)	8.4%

5-Year Holding Period Returns Per Annum for Stocks

Probability of Profitable Investing
Over Any 5-Year Period = 90.2%

Standard & Poor's 500 Total Return Index
Latest 5-Year Period Ending 12/31/98 = 24.0

Monthly Data 12/31/30 - 12/31/98

(MAGNET2)

Courtesy of Ned Davis Research

As we move to five-year holding periods, the odds of being profitable increase to over 90%.

CHART 3-4

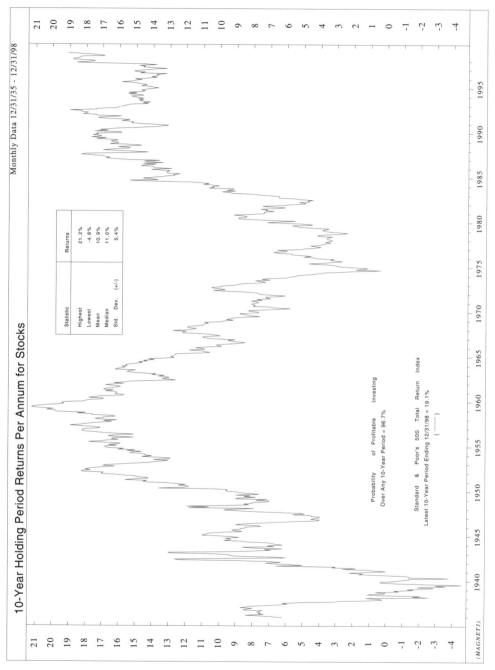

Courtesy of Ned Davis Research

Volatility is further reduced when looking at ten-year holding periods. The odds of being profitable jump to 96%.

CHART 3-5

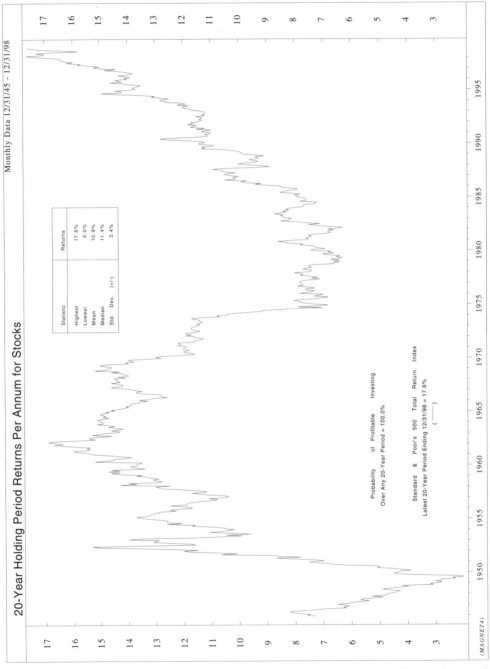

Courtesy of Ned Davis Research

Since 1945 there has not been a single unprofitable twenty-year holding period.

Know Who You Are

*"If you don't know who you are, the stock market
is an expensive place to find out."*
George Goodman, 1959

*"Knowledge born from actual experience is the answer
to why one profits; lack of it is the reason one loses."*
Gerald M. Loeb

*"To make a success, you must study and investigate yourself. Unless you
change from a "lamb" to a thinker and seek knowledge, you will go the way
of all lambs,-to slaughter under the margin caller's axe. Others can only
help you when you help yourself, or show how to help yourself."*
William D. Gann, *Truth of the Stock Tape*

Successful investing requires knowledge, time and commitment, discipline
and patience, and the ability to develop an investment strategy that is
compatible with your personality. First, let's look at some examples of
investment styles that are born from an undefined investment strategy:

- An individual who lacks discipline and adjusts a stock portfolio based upon current news headlines suffers along with his returns.

- An investor who is risk averse may understand that over time stocks have outperformed bonds. But, this same investor may sell stocks at the bottom of a declining market if he misjudged his original risk tolerance.

- Investors unwilling to commit the necessary time and effort in maintaining a portfolio will have marginal investment results.

Knowledge

Each individual must consider what he knows when planning an investment strategy. Recognizing your current level of knowledge, and how you will acquire the additional wisdom you need, are all-important factors.

Time and Commitment

How much time are you willing to spend monitoring your portfolio? This is a critical question. Profitable investing requires time and commitment just like physical body conditioning. If you plan to be in top physical shape, lots of time in the gym, running, or swimming is required to achieve your goal. It would be foolish to think that your financial portfolio could be maintained in the proper shape without the same kind of commitment.

An individual's investment plan should be based on his level of interest in ensuring personal financial success. The more diversified a portfolio is, and the more complex your strategy, the more time you will need. For example, exceptionally rewarding and under-followed stock ideas are only found by those investors willing to take the time to uncover and track them. On the other hand, well-known companies and mutual funds could be monitored more easily. To be successful, an investor must map out a strategy that carefully matches his own personality and level of commitment.

Discipline

Although many investors start with an approach that will work for them, the ability to maintain discipline eludes far too many people. This is caused by a variety of psychological issues, led by fear and greed, that tend to dominate predetermined financial strategies.

During various stages of a stock market, different investment styles will work better than others. Sometimes a value approach will be in favor. Other times a growth or momentum style works better. The key to success is in not switching your own style to accommodate the market.

Usually an individual's personality will prevent him from being equally adept with the various styles of investing. For example, a conservative individual may realize that the market is currently favoring momentum investing. Although the investor is correct with his assessment of the market, there is only a remote likelihood of his effectively managing the active trading that is required in a momentum environment. On the other hand, during a period when the market is more favorable to value style investing, an aggressive and active trader will have an equally difficult time. He will buy into the correct positions, and then lack the patience to own those securities when they actually start to pay off. What's critical is having the discipline to allow enough time for the investment strategy to bear fruit.

A method that may work for some individuals would be the use of mutual funds. Investing in a fund run by a value manager at the right time, and investing in a fund run by a growth manager when growth is in favor, will create excellent results. Even more dramatic results can be achieved with sector funds.

Patience

The last trait for successful investing is patience. Without it, your returns will be more limited. Warren Buffett reminds us that it takes nine months for a woman to deliver a baby. Investments usually take more time to work out than most people consider.

The following shows the most common styles of stock investments, and the time frames expected to reach fruition:

Style of Investment	Timetable
Momentum	Should begin to work quickly, sell on a breakdown of the momentum.
Value	Two to five years for the market to discover the idea.
Turnaround	May take five or more years. Sell only if there is a negative change in the direction or the management of the company.

Once you plan an investment strategy that complements your personality, managing a portfolio should be simple. The challenge will be to follow the game plan and to remain disciplined.

For example, if you invest in a "turnaround" company, your expected time frame needs to be quite lengthy, usually a few years. On the other hand, when buying a momentum style stock, your holding period should only be until the momentum slows. The following chart shows various types of investments and typical holding periods:

INVESTMENT	HOLDING PERIOD
Stocks	
Momentum Stock	Until momentum slows
Value Stock	2-3 years
Turnaround stock	3-5 years
Dividend growth stock	Dividend not raised for 2 years
Bonds	Depending on yield curve
Mutual funds	
Growth funds	10+ years
Bond funds	Depending on yield curve
Sector funds	Depending on economy

An investor who establishes varying time frames for holding different types of securities will be much less inclined to lose patience in well researched ideas. This type of analysis will also assist the investor from "holding too long," while watching his momentum idea fall out of favor and create large losses.

5

Planning:
The First Step

"The people who sustain the worst losses are usually those who overreach. And it's not necessary: Steady, moderate gains will get you where you want to go."

John Train

Proper planning is essential in ensuring profitable investing. Like most major endeavors, those that begin with a well-developed plan, achieve superior results. Building a house requires that many plans be finalized prior to starting construction. Similarly, building a stock portfolio obligates the investor to engage in a tremendous amount of forethought and planning.

There are many questions each investor must ask himself to ensure proper results. Depending on his age, different priorities will dictate the strategies and investments that make the most sense. Someone near retirement may seek income and safety of principal, while a thirty-year-old may be looking for growth of principal and, as such, will be willing to accept more volatility.

The more questions that are addressed in the early stages of the investment process, the better the results. When planning a long trip a good traveler will map out his expected journey. Similarly, a smart investor will use his plan in the same fashion. Answering the following questions should help to create a destination, a time frame to get there, and a compass to maintain the proper direction.

- What is my most pressing need- income or growth?

- How long do I have to achieve my goals?

- How actively do I want to be involved in managing my assets?

- How much volatility can I handle without altering my course?

- What life style changes can I anticipate that may change my priorities?

- Do I want to "go it alone" or use the guidance of a professional?

- How much money will I be able to add to my portfolio, and when?

- How often will I review my plan and results?

Spend the time to reflect on these questions. They will improve your ability to allocate assets, and achieve positive long-term investment results.

The following are two worksheets that I have developed. The first will assist you in determining your general investment objectives. The second will assist investors in monitoring their stocks.

INVESTMENT OBJECTIVES QUESTIONNAIRE
PLEASE CIRCLE CORRECT RESPONSE

1. Does the money to be invested represent all of your liquid assets?

   ☐ Yes   ☐ No

If you answered "no," then how would you summarize the overall liquidity of your assets that could be invested?

   ☐ High   ☐ Medium   ☐ Low

2. Do you expect a specific annual total return for the portfolio?

   ☐ Yes If yes, what is the return?   ☐ No

3. The time you establish to reach your investment objectives is important. The longer the time the more likely that market cycles will average out, improving your chance to meet your goals. What is the approximate time you are willing to keep your funds invested?

   ☐ 1 to 3 years   ☐ 3 to 5 years   ☐ Longer than 5 years

4. Total return is the sum of interest, dividends, and capital appreciation. Generally, the greater the emphasis placed on high income (dividends and interest only), the less potential for capital appreciation. Do you have any specific requirements for annual income to be earned through your investments?

   ☐ Yes. If so, please indicate rate_____% or $_____

   ☐ No

5. Do you plan on withdrawing any cash from your account? The cash amount and frequency of these withdrawals may influence the way you structure your portfolio.

   ☐ No substantial withdrawals in the next five years.

   ☐ Withdrawals will probably be less than contributions during the next five years.

   ☐ Withdrawals may exceed contributions during the next five years.

6. Are there any quality restrictions for the equity and/or fixed income products in your portfolio?

   ☐ Yes   ☐ Major restrictions   ☐ Minor restrictions   ☐ No

If yes, please indicate specific levels such as Moody's Ratings, Standard & Poor's, etc.

7. Are there any constraints on owning any specific security or industry group in the account or any legal or tax issues related to the account's investment holdings?

   ☐ Yes   ☐ No

If yes, please explain.

8. In general, which best fits your overall investment objective? Check one.

   ☐ Growth—Emphasizing greater capital appreciation without income consideration.

   ☐ Growth with income—Equally emphasizing capital appreciation and income.

   ☐ Income—Emphasizing dividend and interest bearing products that also provide some capital appreciation.

   ☐ Preservation of capital—Emphasizing protection of principal with income being considered.

9. Which category best matches your attitude toward investment risk? Choose one.

   ☐ Aggressive: Willing to make investments involving high risk.

   ☐ Moderate: Willing to take some risk.

   ☐ Conservative: Risk averse.

   ☐ Preservation of capital: Emphasizing protection of principal with income considerations.

Stock Selection Checklist

Action: Buy_____ Sell Short_____

Stock Name_____ Industry_____

Number of Shares_____ Price of Stock_____ Amount invested_____

Stop loss_____ Amount willing to loose_____

Ruling Reason for commitment_____

Product or service of company_____

Technical Position

_____Hitting a new high

_____Hugging bullish support

_____Hugging bearish resistance

_____Rolling over from being extended

_____Higher tops & bottoms

_____Lower tops & bottoms

_____Coming off bottom

_____Major pullback in uptrend

_____Pulled back to support

_____Breaking out of base

Other Considerations

_____Relative Strength   _____Resistance

_____EPS   _____Support

_____Accumulation/Distribution

Evolving as an Investor: Developing a Pattern for Success

"There are old traders around and bold traders around but there are no old, bold traders around."

Bob Dinda, Dean Witter

"Become more humble as the market goes your way."

Bernard Baruch

Investing is very much like other life skills- competence develops over time. At first, a lack of experience makes for timid investing, but as confidence grows, bolder strategies can be developed and implemented.

Keep matters as simple as possible in the early stages of investing. Buy stock in companies that you understand. A good place to start might be your favorite chain store, restaurant, or a product you like to use. My first investment was something that was easy for me to understand- H.J. Heinz Co. I knew I liked their ketchup on my hamburger. As simplistic as this sounds, it's a great way for beginners to pick stocks. Open your refrigerator and see what products you like, and be a part owner in the companies that make them.

As you continue to add to your portfolio, it is a good idea to buy stock in a variety of industries. By looking around your home you will undoubtedly find other investment ideas. It may surprise new investors, but corporations that have publicly traded stock manufacture most of your household products. When you decide to buy a product because you really like it, check to see if that company has publicly traded stock. The long-term investment returns in the stock of companies like Clorox (in your laundry room), Sara Lee (in your kitchen), and Black & Decker (in your garage) have been, at times, outstanding.

Obviously, many great investment ideas are less tangible than those made in the stock of consumer product companies. The ability to find these more complex stocks will come with time, as you start to understand the fundamental factors that are involved. For example, management, market share, growth of the industry and profit margins should all be considered. The important lessons learned through earlier investing will help you immensely.

Most people also have a great deal of knowledge in a particular subject area, but few take advantage of their personal expertise. For example, a doctor may have detailed knowledge of a particular medical device manufacturer, through his daily use of that equipment. It would make sense for this doctor to explore the possibility of investing in that company. But in reality, a review of the investment portfolios of most doctors, will show that they own stocks in industries such as oil and gas exploration and real estate. Similarly, you will find real estate professionals that have extensive stock holdings in medical device and biotechnology companies, where their knowledge is limited. It sounds silly, but as a broker, I have seen this many times.

As important as it is to buy stock in a variety of industries, over-diversification is a problem often characteristic of the novice investor. By the very nature of business, not all companies can be great. As your net worth grows with proper management, your available investment capital will mushroom. Your best investments will represent a larger portion of your portfolio and your psychological need to be diversified will be reduced. By this time the balance between adequate diversification and significant positions will be developed, and this is when truly great returns will be achieved.

After many years of profitable investing, an inner confidence develops, and decisions will come more easily. But, regardless of how good your judgment becomes, the bad ideas will still appear in your portfolio from time to time. Hopefully, you will learn to quickly sell poor stock performers and therefore take smaller losses. More importantly, you should be able to hold your real "winners" longer, and realize fantastic gains.

The time frame for each investor's evolution will vary, and the process should not be rushed. The lessons learned over your investment career are invaluable. The rewards will come to those investors patient enough to learn from their prior mistakes, yet persistent enough to overcome the inevitable failures. In evolution, only the strong survive—and survival is not easy.

Like many other crafts, profitable investing takes practice. The skills and knowledge required take time. In his classic book, *The Battle for Investment Survival,* Gerald M. Loeb brings this point to light. He theorizes that only by opening and closing transactions, can you acquire the judgment needed to be a profitable investor. The simple act of trading will not, however, lead to better judgment. It is the careful analysis and self study of the decisions made in those trades that will create a clearer understanding of both the markets, and your own ability to manage your emotions. In other professions it is called practice. In the field of investing, experience has no parallel.

Investing is difficult to master, so practice (experience) is always required. I have never met an individual who consistently makes profitable investment decisions. Michael Burke, who runs a great investment service, *Investor's Intelligence,* terms this process "paying tuition to the school of knowledge." Most successful investors have paid more tuition in the early stages of their investment career than one can imagine. When asked, Mr. Burke will remind investors that no matter how extensive your experience, you are never finished making new mistakes. The truly great investors use these mistakes as learning experiences. Those people who are unwilling to face their errors, and learn from them, are destined to be mediocre investors, at best.

How many professions offer an opportunity to make true fortunes? Are these professions dominated by individuals simply because they possess talent? When you think about this, it is obvious that practice and commitment are also required to bring people to the top of their field.

The financial markets humble many individuals who simply underestimate the complexities of these markets, and their inability to manage their emotions. Others learn from their mistakes. Some people are lucky enough to achieve financial success through the markets because they are able to harness their intellect, emotions, and their experiences to develop a pattern of success. It pays to study these individuals closely. Then, take your observations to the market, and develop your own profitable path.

7

Understanding Bonds

"The best time to buy long-term bonds is when
short-term rates are higher than long-term rates."
George Soros

"$1,000 left to earn interest at 8% will grow to $43 quadrillion
in 400 years, but the first hundred years are the hardest."
Sidney Homer, Salomon Brothers

Despite this book's emphasis on stocks and stock selection, many investors keep a portion of their assets in fixed-income investments. Accordingly, I am devoting a few pages to this subject to review some common misconceptions.

Bonds are the largest component of the asset class known as fixed-income securities. Each investor's risk tolerance level will determine to whom he is willing to lend money, and the level of confidence he has in the borrower's ability to repay. When one buys a Certificate of Deposit (CD) at a bank, the purchaser is investing in the simplest example of a fixed-income security. An agreement is made to loan your money to the bank for a speci-fied time period and for a specific percentage return.

Early in my Wall Street career I spent almost five years exclusively buy-ing and trading bonds for my clients. I also purchased bonds for my own portfolio. During this period I learned many important subtleties about bonds that helped to improve my clients' timing and profitability.

I came to the conclusion that most bond investors receive surprisingly poor returns. While bonds are perceived as a safe investment, they actually carry many different types of risks (see Chapter 8). First, they lose to the silent killer- inflation. Over time, the effects of inflation erode a bond-holder's purchasing power. Chart 7-1 demonstrates this quite clearly. One dollar in 1960 is now worth only 18 cents after adjusting for inflation. In addition, bonds have historically generated significantly lower returns as compared to common stocks. Considering all these facts, I soon liquidated my bond portfolio, and redirected my attention to the stock market.

I do not believe that inflation has been tamed. In fact I am convinced that today's low "reported" inflation statistics are grossly understated. This is because food and energy are underweighted in the Consumer Price In-dex (CPI), while housing is overweighted. Regardless of the exact annual inflation numbers, a large allocation of investment money in bonds will certainly do damage to one's future purchasing power. This is shown in Chart 7-2. One dollar in 1930 is now worth only 11 cents after adjusting for inflation.

Another reason investors get poor results with bonds is because of the effects of interest rates on bond prices. Bond prices move inversely with interest rates, so when interest rates rise, bond prices fall, and vice versa. Let's use an example of an individual who entered into a contract to lend someone money several years ago at an interest rate of 8%. If current inter-est rate contracts are 12%, and the investor wants to sell their 8% agree-ment to someone else, that contract will be deemed undesirable. If however, current interest rates fell to 5%, the 8% contract would be very desirable and could be resold at a premium price. For the duration of the bond, the price will continue to fluctuate to reflect the change in current interest rates.

Bonds are issued with various lengths of maturity. The longer the bond's maturity, the greater the price will fluctuate with changes in interest rates. Therefore, one needs to consider future interest rates in the timing and purchase of bonds. The best time to purchase bonds is just prior to a downturn in long- and short-term interest rates.

A yield curve can be obtained by plotting the interest rates that bonds are paying at various lengths of maturity. This is shown in most financial periodicals, and studied by bond traders. Normally, the longer the maturity of a bond, the higher the interest rate it pays. This is because the issuer is forced to pay a higher rate for the privilege of holding your money over a time period in which rates may fluctuate a great deal.

An issuer of bonds may believe that interest rates will soon fall. In this case, he will issue bonds with high yields for shorter duration, and lower yields for the longer duration. Under this scenario, when the short-term bonds mature, bonds with lower interest rates can be issued at great savings to the issuer.

When short-term bonds are paying a higher interest rate than longer-term bonds, an inverted yield curve is created. This is a condition in which investors and traders should buy long term bonds. Interests rates will likely drop and produce capital gains for the investor.

Table 7-1 shows yields and various yields to maturity on zero coupon bonds.

The following are some common municipal bond terms:

Accrued Interest: Coupon interest accumulated on a bond or note since the last interest payment or, for a new issue, from the dated date (original date of issue) to the date of delivery.

Basis Point: One one-hundredth of one percent.

Blue Sky Law: A legal term referring to various state laws enacted to protect the public against securities fraud. These laws describe the method and form of registration of municipal bonds in each particular state.

Current Yield: The ratio of the coupon rate on a bond to the dollar purchase price, expressed as a percentage.

Dated Date: The date carried on the face of a bond or note from which interest normally begins to accrue.

Default: The failure to pay principal and/or interest when due, or a breach of the agreement.

Double Barreled Bond: A bond with two distinct pledged sources of revenue such as earmarked moneys from a specific source or aid payments, as well as the general obligation taxing powers of the issuer.

Good Delivery: The physical delivery of bonds upon sale, which fulfills all legal requirements necessary for the change of ownership.

Negotiated Sale: The sale of a bond issue where an underwriter(s) negotiates the terms and conditions of the sale with the bond buyers, on behalf of an issuer.

Original Issue Discount: A bond issued at an offering price substantially below par; the appreciation from the original price to par over the life of the bonds is treated as tax-exempt income.

Price to Call: The yield of a bond priced to the first call date rather than maturity.

Refunding Bond: The issuance of a new bond for the purpose of retiring an already outstanding bond issue.

Sinking Fund: Money set aside on a periodic basis to retire term bonds at or prior to maturity.

Taxable Equivalent Yield: The yield an investor would have to obtain on a taxable corporate or U.S. government bond to match the same after tax yield on a municipal bond.

Trading Flat: Bonds that trade at their principal amount with no accrued interest included, usually in default.

Zero Coupon Bonds: Zero coupons bonds allow investors to compound their principal over time, but pay no cash dividends. The current value of these bonds is quite volatile and often misunderstood by investors.

In summary, bonds, because of their complexity, represent the category of investment that is least understood when making asset allocation decisions, the subject of the next chapter. Those interested in learning more about bonds are encouraged to read *The Handbook of Fixed Income Securities* by Frank J. Fabozzi.

Table 7-1. YIELDS ON ZERO COUPON BONDS

Years To Maturity	Yield To Maturity										
	5.00%	5.50%	6.00%	6.50%	7.00%	7.50%	8.00%	8.50%	9.00%	9.50%	10%
30	$227	$196	$170	$147	$127	$110	$95	$82	$71	$62	$54
25	290	258	228	202	179	159	141	125	111	98	87
20	372	338	307	278	253	229	208	189	172	156	142
18	411	377	345	316	290	266	244	223	205	188	173
16	454	420	388	359	333	308	285	264	244	227	210
14	501	468	437	408	382	357	333	312	292	273	255
12	553	521	492	464	438	413	390	369	348	328	310
10	610	581	554	527	503	479	456	435	415	395	377
9	641	614	587	562	538	515	494	473	453	434	416
8	674	648	623	599	577	555	534	514	494	476	458
7	708	684	661	639	618	597	577	558	540	522	505
6	744	722	701	681	662	643	625	607	590	573	557
5	781	762	744	726	709	692	676	659	644	629	614
4	821	805	789	774	759	745	731	717	703	690	677
3	862	850	837	825	813	802	790	779	768	757	746
2	906	897	888	880	871	864	855	847	839	831	823
1	952	947	943	938	933	929	925	920	916	911	907

Courtesy of MAGNET® Management LLC

You can use this table to determine the approximate value of a zero coupon bond. For example, a $100,000 bond yeilding 7%, with ten years to maturity, would have a present value of $50,300.

CHART 7-1

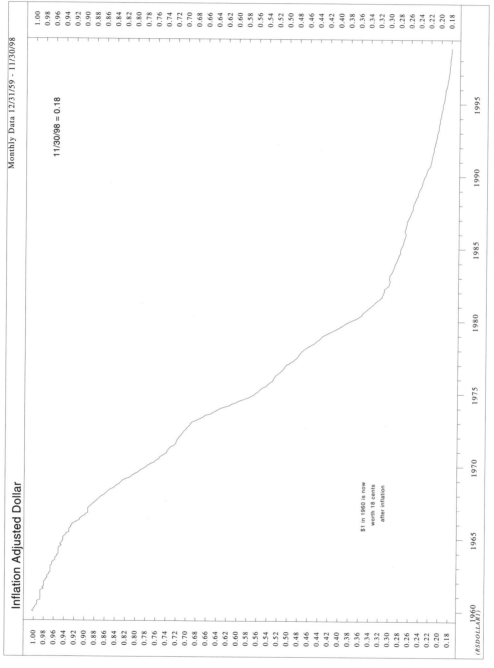

Monthly Data 12/31/59 - 11/30/98

11/30/98 = 0.18

Inflation Adjusted Dollar

$1 in 1960 is now worth 18 cents after inflation

Courtesy of Ned Davis Research

Inflation is one of your worst enemies and a fixed income portfolio will lose the battle against inflation.

CHART 7-2

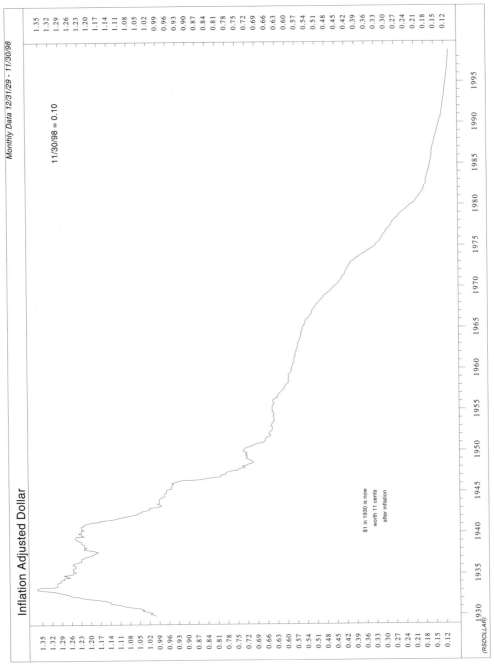

Courtesy of Ned Davis Research

One real secret to investing is generating the best "after inflation" returns.

Asset Allocation

"Don't put your eggs in one basket."
Market Maxim

"Put your eggs in one basket and watch the basket."
An alternate strategy

"In investing, the return you want should depend on whether you want to eat well or sleep well."
J. Kenfield Morley

The process of diversifying an investment portfolio among stocks, bonds, and cash is the topic of asset allocation. A portfolio may also include other holdings like real estate and collectibles (art, jewelry, exotic cars, etc.). This book will only address the diversification among financial assets.

The subject of asset allocation has become increasingly popular in recent years. Most theories have been highly mathematical, with an emphasis on the maximization of total return based on the proper blend of stocks, bonds, and cash. Unfortunately there is no mathematical formula that incorporates the emotions of the individual investor while he watches his portfolio fluctuate over time. The subject of asset allocation would be an extremely easy topic if the emotional aspect were removed. Although history is only a guide, Chart 8-1 on Page 45 shows the rates of return of the various asset classes since 1926.

In Charles D. Ellis' and James R. Vertin's book, *Classics: An Investor's Anthology,* investment returns are compared and discussed in several articles written by various authors. This book is a "must read" for those with a serious interest in investing. In another Ellis book, *Investment Policy,* the author addresses the topic of asset allocation. Although this book's primary emphasis is on asset allocation and issues that arise in the management of pension funds, they approximate the same issues that apply to individuals.

It is commonly stated that risk and reward are inseparable. Perhaps a more accurate statement would be that volatility and reward are inseparable. An investment in a short term Treasury Note has very little volatility. However an investment in Treasury Notes could hardly be considered a safe investment when the effects of inflation are considered.

While some consider stocks risky and bonds safe, every investor should weigh the various types of risk associated with different asset classes. Here are some definitions of the most common risks found in investing.

Market Risk: The uncertainty of how the market will value an investment asset at any given point in time. This is the kind of risk most people think about. Market risk includes fluctuation and volatility of prices, and the possibility of losing the full investment (i.e. there is no longer a market for the security you purchased).

Inflation Risk: This is the risk associated with earning a positive rate of return on your investments but still eroding your purchasing power. The rate of return on investment assets must be greater than inflation. Inflation risk is much less discussed but has severe consequences to many fixed income investors. (See Chapter 7)

Interest Rate Risk: Rising interest rates will usually cause market values to decline; thereby causing fixed income securities and some equities to lose their value.

Credit Risk: This is primarily associated with investments in bonds. It involves the possibility that the issuer of a fixed income security will default and be unable to pay the principal and interest stated in the original terms of the bond.

Liquidity Risk: Sometimes an asset cannot be converted to cash when needed. This is more common in investments other than registered securities.

Tax Risk: This occurs when a change in the tax laws reduces the market value of an investment. For example, real estate investments were hurt badly in the 1980's when the tax laws were changed. The municipal bond market continues to be threatened by changes in the tax code that would affect their tax-exempt status, although this is unlikely to occur.

Reinvestment Risk: This risk is associated with fixed income securities. It considers the possibility that maturing investments will be reinvested at lower rates of return. Those owning bonds or bank deposits that paid high rates of interest in the early 1980's became painfully aware of this risk in recent years.

You can see why risk is such an important concept to incorporate in developing an investment strategy, and in avoiding many of the pitfalls that investors encounter.

I have read many financial studies proving that a diversified portfolio of highly volatile investments will likely generate a large return if held over a long period of time. This volatility would be acceptable because it would yield a higher long-term return. The conclusion is that the best investment returns will be generated when stocks represent the highest percentage of one's portfolio, provided the investor can still sleep during a severe market downturn. This is brought to light in Charts 8-2 and 8-3 on Pages 46 and 47 that clearly show that long term holding periods should not be cut short because they incorporate periods of severe declines and subsequent advances.

As a broker I have found that individuals overestimate their ability to emotionally accept a market downturn, as many nervous investors inevitably sell at low points. This is where the process of establishing a comfortable asset allocation is helpful. An investor that has carefully planned his portfolio and established time horizons (see next two chapters) is less likely to panic during market volatility. Therefore, I believe that asset allocation is more a matter of personal preference than a mathematical endeavor. This subject will come under more careful scrutiny as the stock market shows signs of downside pressure.

This chart shows how each risk category applies individually to the stock and bond market.

Table 8-1 Risks of Stocks and Bonds

Type of Risk	Stocks	Bonds
Market Risk	Significant risk. Stocks can fluctuate greatly over the short term.	Can be moderated by sticking with short maturities.
Inflation Risk	Can be moderated by maintaining a healthy portfolio	Significant risk. Greatest enemy of all bond investors.
Interest Rate Risk	Generally, stocks perform better during low interest rate environments.	Significant risk. Bond values are inversely related to interest rates.
Credit Risk	Extremely low.	Can be moderated by trading in Treasuries.
Liquidity Risk	Can be moderated by trading in active stocks.	Extremely low.
Tax Risk	Does not apply.	Extremely low.
Reinvestment Risk	Does not apply.	Works against investors during decreasing rate environment.

Chart 8-1

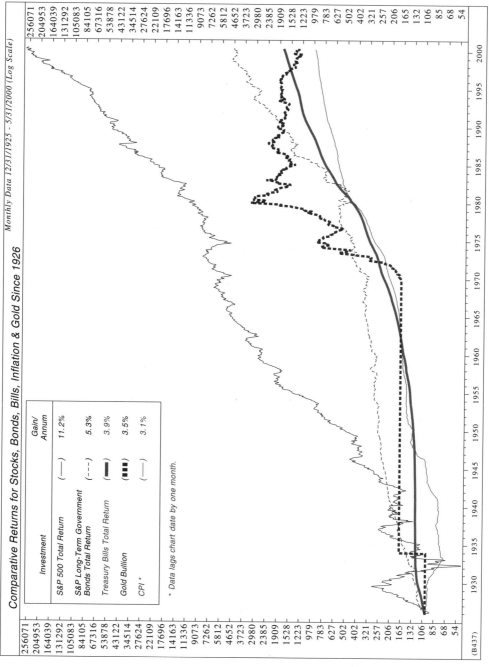

A long-term look at the returns from various asset groups helps show the dramatic overperformance of the stock market as compared to fixed income securities.

Chart 8-2

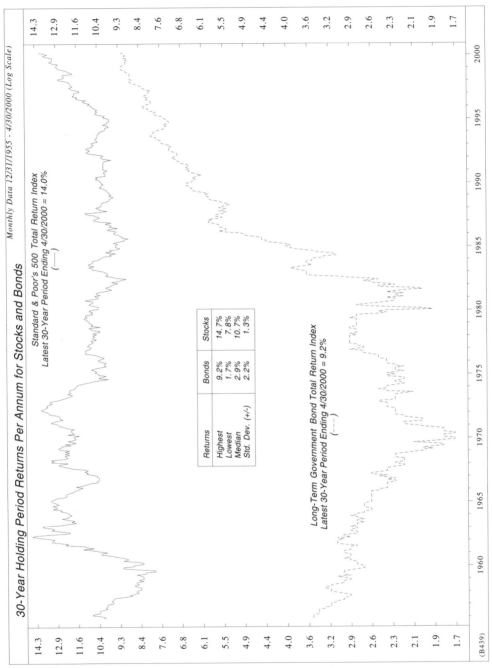

The disparity in the "rolling returns" generated in stocks versus bonds speaks volumes in favor of long term investing in stocks.

Chart 8-3

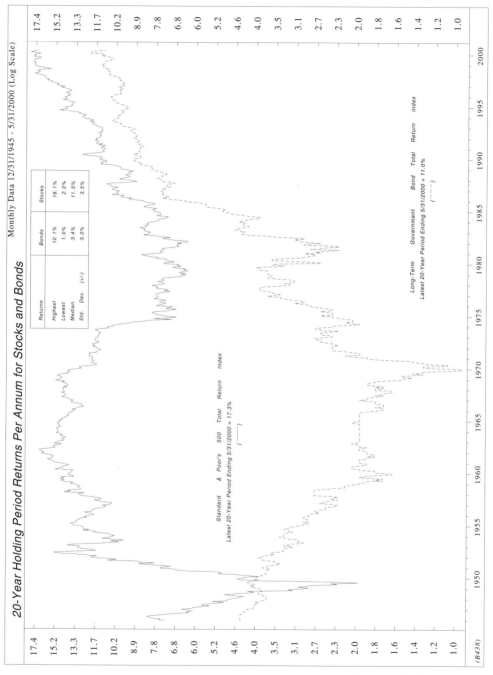

Courtesy of Ned Davis Research

The 8% differential between the median return in stocks versus bonds is very significant when returns are compounded.

9

When to Buy and Sell

"It is no coincidence that three of the top five stock options traders in a recent trading contest were all ex-Marines."
Robert Prechter, Jr., Elliott Wave Theorist

"Wall Street has a uniquely hysterical way of thinking the world will end tomorrow but be fully recovered in the long run, then a few years later believing the immediate future is rosy but that the long term stinks."
Kenneth L. Fisher, *Wall Street Waltz*

"Trend is begun by an explosion in price. The resulting new trend stays in effect until there is a new explosion in the opposite direction."
Larry Williams, *Long Term Secrets to Short Term Trading*

Timing is everything. While this old Wall Street adage is applied to many facets of life, it is most applicable in the field of investing. Careful fundamental research will answer the question of "what to buy," but both short-term traders and long term investors must master the art of "when" to buy and sell, in order to trade successfully. There are hosts of technical trading tools that facilitate the "when," and I have experimented with most of them with varying degrees of success. In this chapter I will outline several of the tools I use most frequently in identifying MAGNET® stocks. If used properly and diligently, these technical tools will greatly enhance your investment returns when combined with fundamental analysis.

Many current statistical computer packages include the following technical (and fundamental) tools:

Moving Averages: As a market advances, the shorter-term moving average will rise above a longer-term moving average. As this faster moving average crosses the slower moving average, a buy signal is generated. In market declines, the shorter-term moving average will cross the longer-term moving average. A sell signal is generated as the shorter-term moving average falls below the longer-term moving average.

MACD (Moving Averages Converging Diverging): The MACD indicator includes a third moving average that forms a trigger line. Whenever this trigger line is crossed, the system generates a trade signal. Whenever the MACD falls below the trigger line, a short call is made. Whenever the MACD crosses above the trigger line, a long call is made.

Stochastics: Long signals occur when the stochastic oscillator moves below a lower level of +20 and then moves back up through the same level. Short signals occur as the stochastic oscillator moves above an upper level of +80 and then falls back through this same level.

Relative Strength: The Relative Strength Index is defined to oscillate between 0 and 100. Typically, 70 is considered an overbought level, and 30 is considered an oversold level. In the relative strength method of trading system, when the index crosses through 70, peaks, and then crosses through 70 again, a short signal occurs. The system generates a long signal whenever the index falls below 30, forms a valley, and rises back through 30.

Volume Analysis: If volume rises for five days in a row and is accompanied by rising stock price, then an upward trend is detected. The system will generate a long call. If volume rises for five days in a row and is accompanied by falling stock price, a downward trend is detected and the system generates a bearish, short call.

Point & Figure Charts: For a pure look at the supply/demand equation of a stock, Point and Figure charts graphically identify breakout and breakdowns. When you get down to it, what is more important then supply vs. demand?

Insider Trading: Tracking insider trading (buying is more important then selling), you get more of a feel and less of a mathematical model to work from.

In his book, *Trading for a Living,* Dr. Alexander Elder describes many of these tools, in detail, and provides examples of each.

I use a service called Telescan™ to access this technical data via my modem/computer. While I have found Telescan to be the best service, there are other packages available as well. It would be hard to imagine an investor who was able to complete a thorough stock analysis without one of these programs.

I also like to use Point & Figure charting. Michael Burke at Chartcraft and Tom Dorsey of Dorsey Wright Associates are two of the leading practitioners of Point & Figure charting. They have both written books on the subject respectively titled *Point & Figure Construction and Formation* and *Point & Figure Charting,* and I would encourage all investors to read these. Point & Figure charts provide market direction, and attempt to measure basic supply and demand. In addition, emphasis is placed on the relative position of each sector within the market. Because sector rotation has become so important over the last few years, understanding this technical tool is critical. Chart 9-19 is an example of Point & Figure.

I perform the following technical analysis to assist me in timing stock purchases:

1. Assess the general direction of the market.

2. Determine the strength of the sector of the stock that I am evaluating.

3. Uncover oversold or overbought conditions, depending on my goals, i.e., going long or selling short.

While I attempt to eliminate my emotions from the process, I make sure to use my experience and judgment with each investment decision. A top technical trader once told me that investing was similar to hunting, and that he had one of the best hunting dogs alive. However, as good a dog as he had, he still did not put the gun in the dog's hands. He used his own judgment in deciding when to fire his weapon. This is a great analogy to why technical analysis should be used in conjunction with other stock selection methodologies. I do not believe in pure mechanical trading. If it worked, computers could be programmed to trade and make fortunes. Profitable trading takes lots of work, and the rewards are commensurate with the effort.

The following charts demonstrate general market timing methods.

CHART 9-1

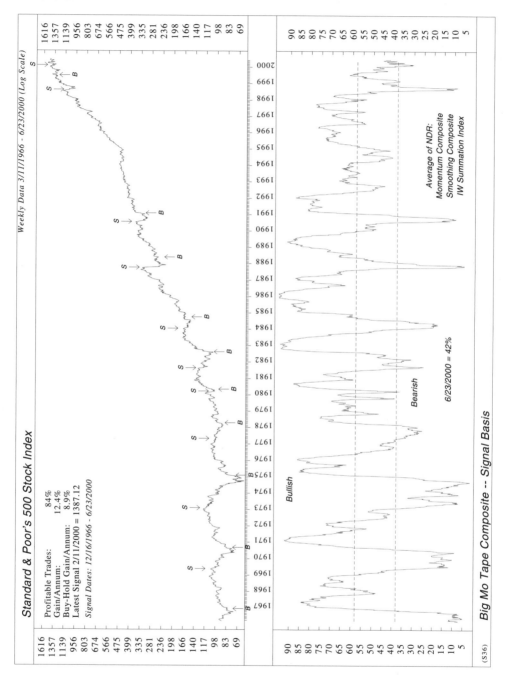

Courtesy of Ned Davis Research

Ned Davis' "Big Mo" is rightfully one of Wall Street's most watched indicators, especially by the institutions. The 84% profitable trades record is truly outstanding.

CHART 9-2

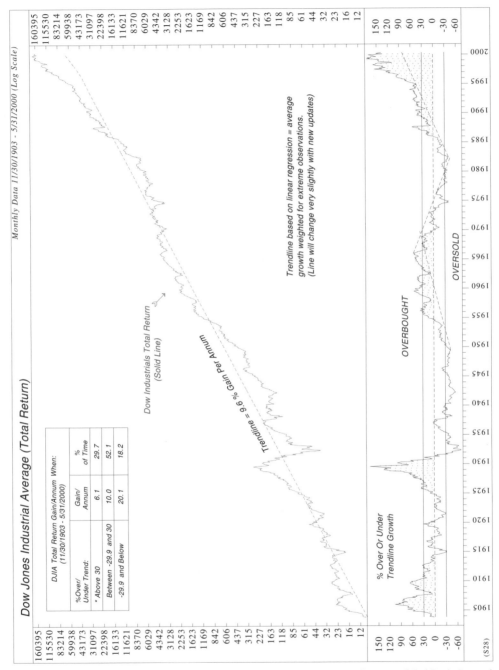

Courtesy of Ned Davis Research

"Regression to the mean" studies are powerful. The bull market that we have witnessed since the 1980's has created an overbought reading matched only by the "Roaring 20's."

CHART 9-3

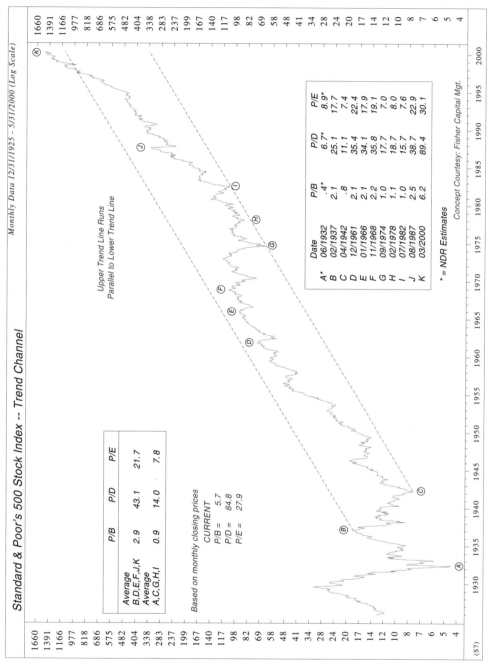

Courtesy of Ned Davis Research

Trend channel analysis helps identify the tops and bottoms of the theoretical envelopes. This highlights another reason for caution in today's market.

CHART 9-4

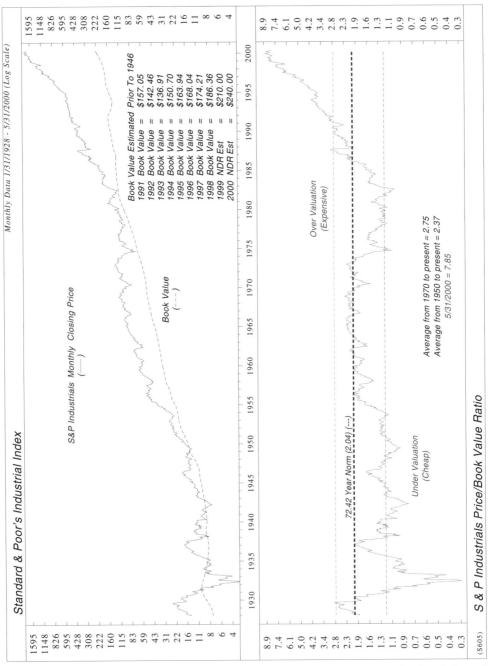

Courtesy of Ned Davis Research

When charted, fundamental data such as the S&P/Book Value ratio present a great picture of the current "relative value" of the market. The progression into the information age and away from the "big plant industrials" have led many experts to discredit this indicator, but I like to look at all data.

CHART 9-5

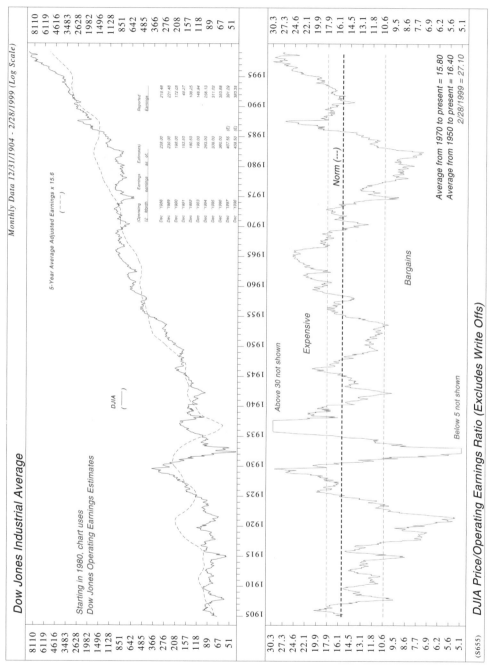

Courtesy of Ned Davis Research

Over the long term, earnings do matter. The proliferation of mergers and one-time "write-offs," along with high investor confidence, has led to a market as "expensive" as we have ever seen. Magnet's focus is on top-line revenue growth.

CHART 9-6

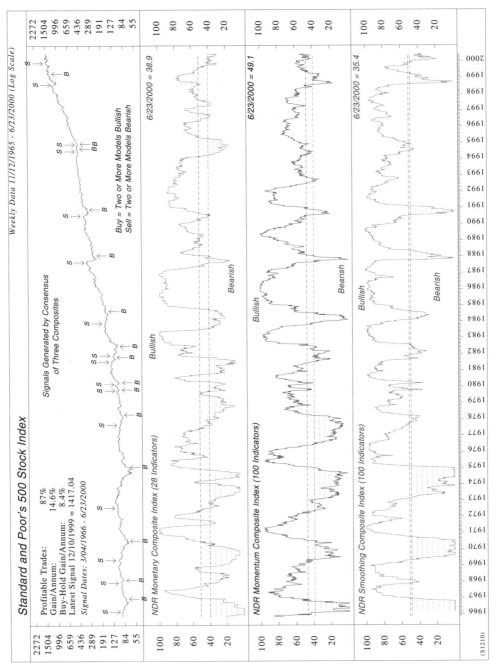

Courtesy of Ned Davis Research

Ned Davis puts it all together in this composite series of graphs. The blend of all these indicators has led to a remarkable 87% "profitable trade" record. This should give the "random walk" followers something to think about.

The following are several charts of individual stocks that also highlight the importance of timing.

CHART 9-7

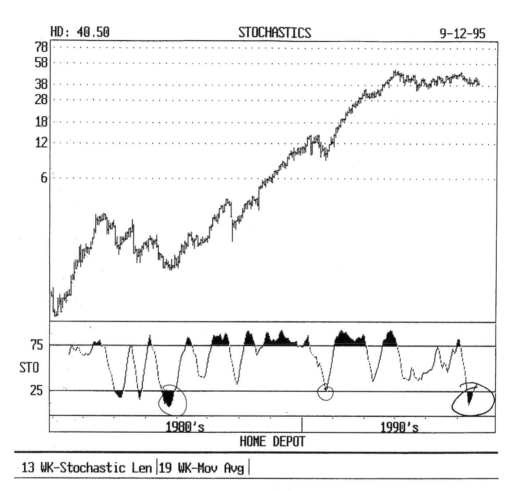

Courtesy of Telescan, Inc.

After a tremendous run in the 1980's, Home Depot share price was flat for over five years. I saw another opportunity to purchase the stock when it became "long term oversold" for only the third time in fifteen years. This was a great buy signal.

CHART 9-8

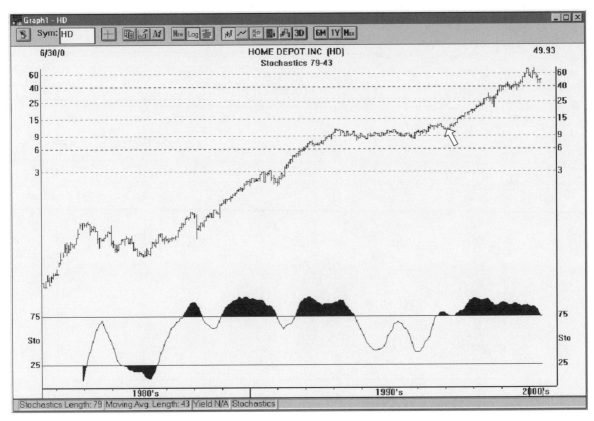

Courtesy of Telescan, Inc.

This buy signal on Home Depot led to a huge return. Same company, very different returns from 1990-1995 versus 1995-2000.

CHART 9-9

Courtesy of Telescan, Inc.

A downtrend in the stock of Alliance Capital was broken when it began an uptrend that lasted over six months. This combination of a strong fundamental company with an improving technical chart is what we look for in selecting MAGNET® stocks.

CHART 9-10

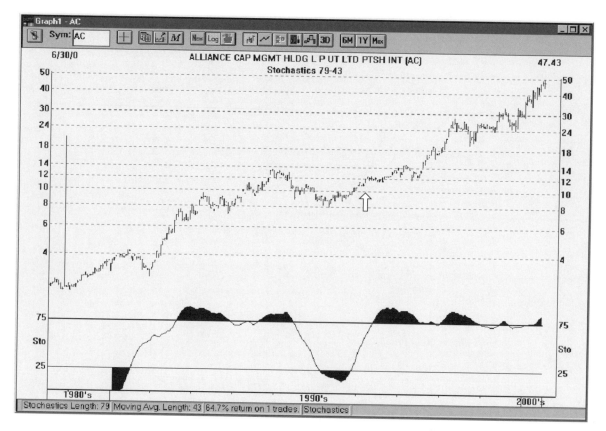

Once Alliance Capital's price momentum began, it turned into one of the premiere stocks of the 1990's.

CHART 9-11

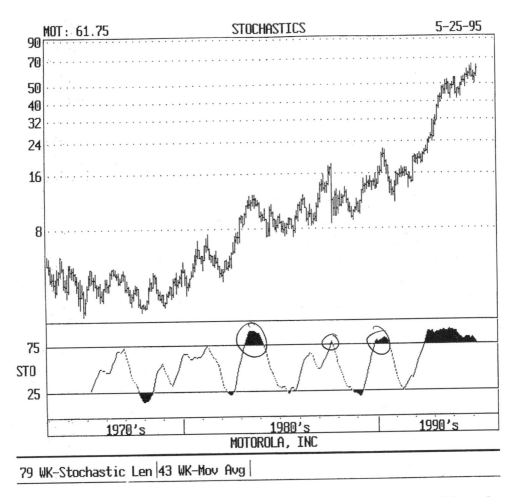

Courtesy of Telescan, Inc.

Despite being a premiere growth stock, Motorola has been subjected to substantial sell-offs in price. Here the long-term stochastics give a loud warning to stay clear of this one, even during a bull market.

CHART 9-12

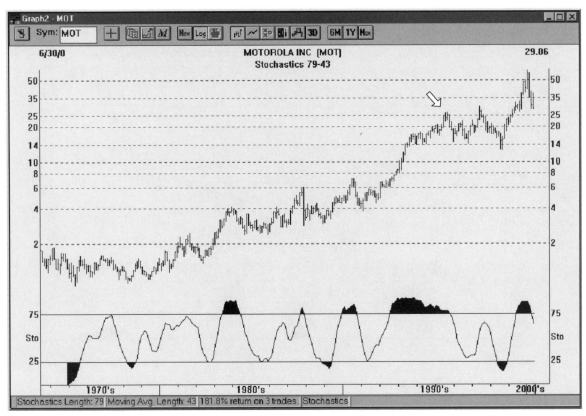

Courtesy of Telescan, Inc.

Motorola dropped by nearly 50% following this "overbought" condition in 1995. Four years later investors still had not made any money, as Motorola sat out a bull market.

CHART 9-13

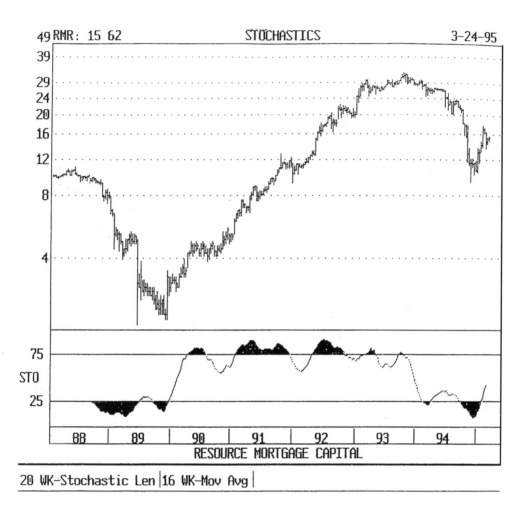

Courtesy of Telescan, Inc.

Following a sharp sell-off in 1994, the long-term stochastics flashed a "second chance" to trade Resource Mortgage Capital, again leading to spectacular returns. See Appendix C for the first buy. (Formerly RAC Mortgage and later Dynex Capital.)

CHART 9-14

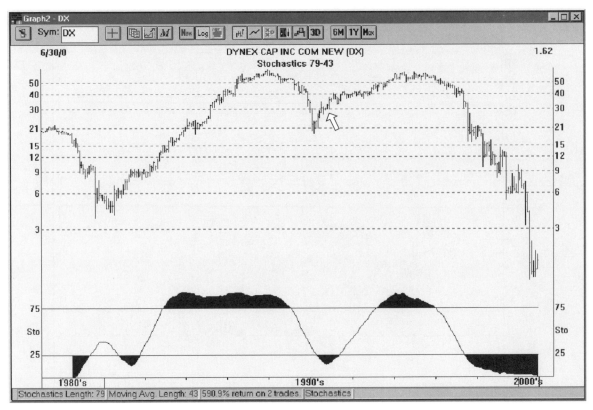

Courtesy of Telescan, Inc.

This long term chart shows that while great trades could have been executed at Resource Mortgage Capital (name changed to Dynex Capital), a long-term "buy and hold" strategy did not work.

CHART 9-15

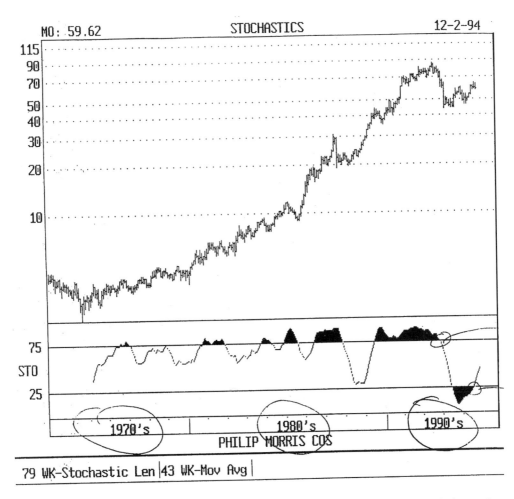

Courtesy of Telescan, Inc.

Long-term investors in Philip Morris have been rewarded handsomely. By using long-term stochastics, you can locate reasonable price entry points into the very best companies. When the long-term stochastics turned up from oversold on this chart, Philip Morris was clearly a "buy." But follow the next three pages.

CHART 9-16

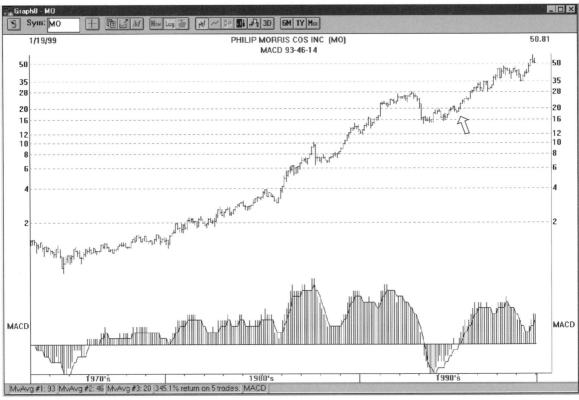

Courtesy of Telescan, Inc.

If you had purchased Philip Morris stock at this "buy" signal, it would have represented a great investment.

CHART 9-17

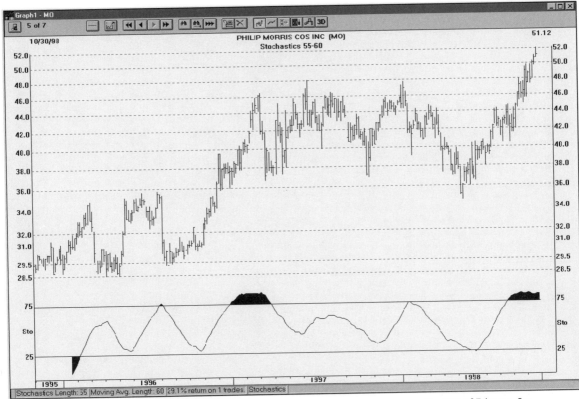

Courtesy of Telescan, Inc.

Using long-term charts with stochastics can help you answer the 'when to buy" question. Despite being an excellent company, this was not a good time to buy Philip Morris. A poor entry point makes it hard to hold even good companies.

CHART 9-18

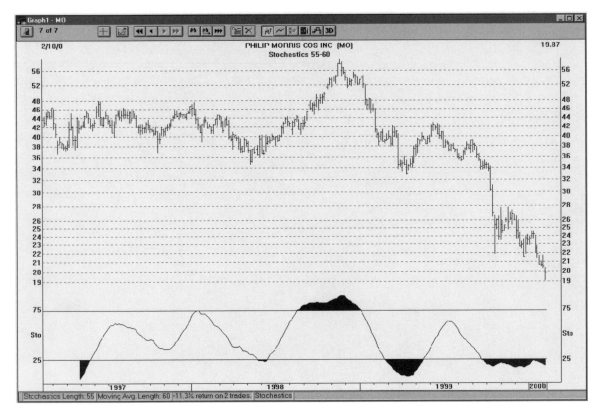

Courtesy of Telescan, Inc.

Just a year later, as a result of highly publicized tobacco lawsuits, Philip Morris is back in an oversold position- according to the stochastics. The ability to utilize unemotional technical indicators gives an investor more information than most media coverage.

CHART 9-19

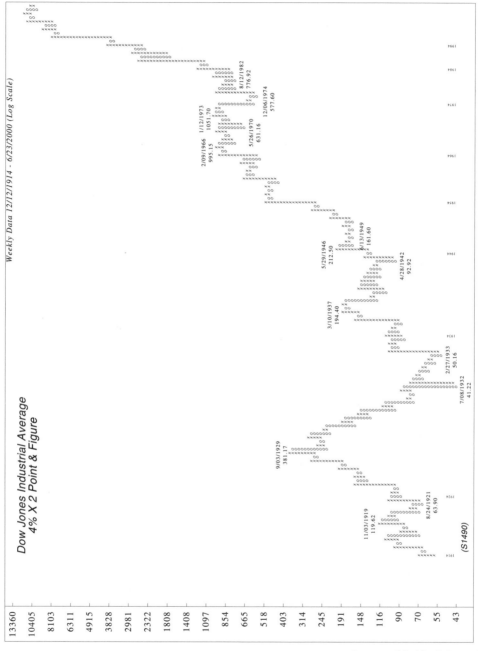

Courtesy of Ned Davis Research

Point and Figure charting often puts complex information into clear perspective. The breakout of an extended base in the early 1980's gave way to a huge upward movement in the Dow. The current position of the Dow is extended and being carried by momentum.

10

Owning Companies: Buy and Hold

"Buy a stock the way you would buy a house. Understand and like it such that you'd be content to own it in the absence of any market."

Warren Buffett

One of the most profitable ways to invest is to buy stocks in great companies and hold them. Think of this as partial ownership in a company over years, business cycles, and perhaps even generations.

Often people discuss the stock market as if they were talking about a trip to a gambling casino. "I'll take a shot with this" or "I feel lucky with that." This thought process prevents individuals from accumulating wealth through the stock market. Ask yourself, "do I want to be a part owner of a company?" If the answer is "yes," you are on the right track to a successful investment. After you identify a specific company, you then need to decide on an acceptable purchase price.

A company whose stock price moves up and down with the economy is called a cyclical stock, and I tend to avoid them. Growth companies, those that are able to expand from one business cycle to the next, offer the best prospects for long-term appreciation.

There are currently some well-known investment experts, most notably Warren Buffett and Peter Lynch, who emphasize buying into companies that you understand, and then sitting back and owning them indefinitely. It is not surprising that they have had such astounding results in the stock market. If it is so simple, then why is it so hard to follow this strategy? The answer is that most investors lack knowledge, and more importantly patience, as discussed in earlier chapters.

It takes time (and sometimes luck) to identify a truly superior company. Once that company is found and your profits begin to accumulate, this investment should be held indefinitely. You should only consider selling if there is a materially significant change in the company's strategy, or the industry outlook.

It only requires a handful of long-term profits in outstanding companies to create personal independent wealth. On the other hand, it will take an unusually large number of small profits to really make a difference over time. So while it is true that no one goes broke taking profits, it is also true that those who allow their profits to compound will be rewarded with significant wealth.

Under ideal circumstances, these long-term holdings will pay for your children's college education, or could be sold in small pieces to pay bills in your retirement years. Ideally, these investments will be passed on to your heirs (without capital gains taxes) or donated to charities. It is this style of investing that I refer to as "owning companies." Remember, you only need a couple of these to make a difference.

Charts 10-1 through 10-4 on Pages 75 to 78 represent the sad truth of taking small profits versus holding great companies for longer time periods. We use Dell Computer Corporation and International Business Machines (IBM) as examples.

CHART 10-1

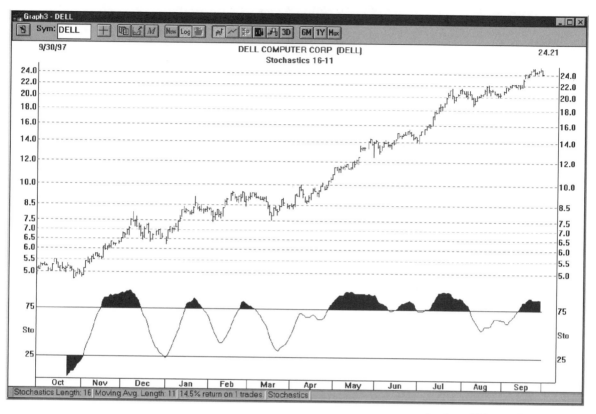

From October 1996 through March 1997 Dell Computer was producing many stochastic "buy" and "sell" signals that led to profitable trades. In this case, however, it is difficult to imagine any short-term trader good enough to beat the "buy and hold" strategy.

CHART 10-2

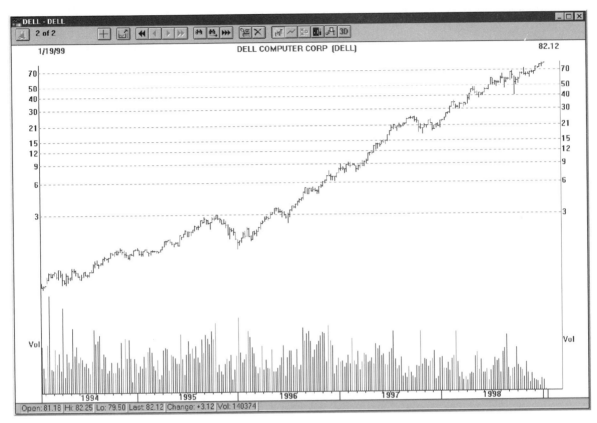

Courtesy of Telescan, Inc.

By taking a longer view of Dell's magnificent run (1994-1998), it is clear that when you find a true industry and market leader, it makes sense to avoid the short-term technical signals. But remember to monitor your investments for changes in company strategy or industry outlook.

CHART 10-3

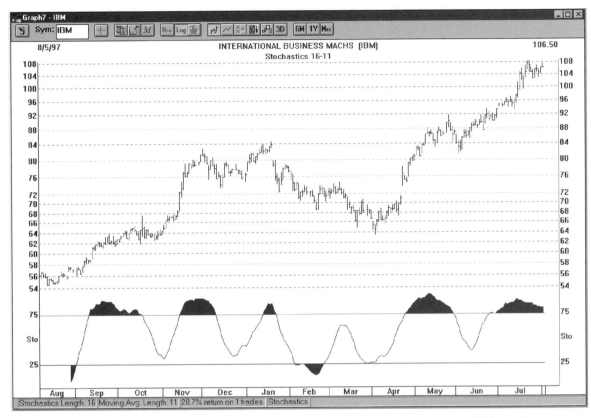

Courtesy of Telescan, Inc.

Technical indicators can often pull you out of a stock too early. Notice the number of stochastic sell signals given by IBM during the uptrend move in 1996-97.

CHART 10-4

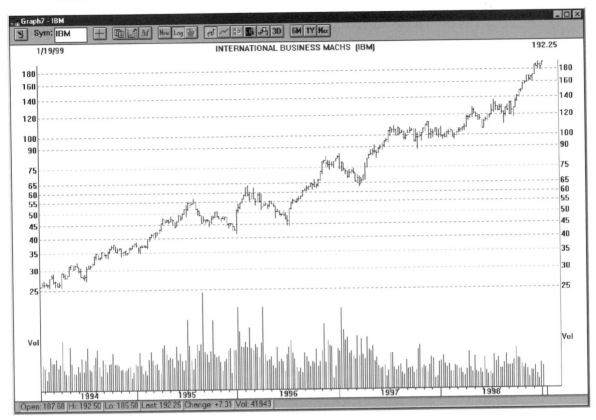

Courtesy of Telescan, Inc.

By looking at a longer-term chart of IBM (1994-1998), it is obvious that a "trigger happy" short-term trader may have made some profitable trades on IBM stock during this stretch. However, the real money was made by holding IBM during this powerful move.

CHAPTER

11

Profitable Portfolio Management: Learn from Your Mistakes

"Good judgment is usually the result of experience and experience is frequently the result of bad judgment."
Robert Lovell Quoted by Robert Sobel, *Panic on Wall Street*

"The price of a stock varies inversely with the thickness of its research file."
Martin Sosnoff

"The new lamb should know that failing to place a stop loss order and overtrading have been the cause of over 90% of the failures in Wall Street. Therefore, in order to make a success he must act in a way to overcome the weak points which have caused ruin in others."
William D. Gann, author of *Truth of the Stock Tape*, and master technician

Profitable investing is one of life's most challenging endeavors because there seems to be an infinite number of potential mistakes. This is the subject of Gerald Loeb's classic, *The Battle for Investment Survival*. The truly successful investor will study each investment transaction, in an attempt to learn from both the successes as well as the failures. Human behavior has us avoid looking back at our failures despite the valuable lessons they offer. The investor that takes the time to review the psychological underpinning of prior decisions will ultimately be able to side step the same potential pitfalls that will appear in the future.

Unfortunately, even the most studious and diligent investor will not eliminate all mistakes, but the conscious decision to avoid repeating the same mistakes makes the difference in the long run. An analogy to the game of chess is helpful here. A novice chess player (like a novice investor) is unlikely to fare well against a tough competitor (the market). The player who takes the game seriously and learns from his mistakes will be the one who shows the fastest improvement.

Understanding why a mistake was made is often as revealing as the mistake itself. The chart below shows the connection between a few common investment mistakes and the psychological motivation behind each one:

Investment Mistake	Psychology
Buy a hot tip	Need to be included
Buy spontaneously	Lack of effort in research
Buy a hot favorite	Need for group approval
Sell too soon	Lack of patience
Hold too long	Unwilling to take action
Average down in a loser	Unwilling to admit mistake

Think of a portfolio like a well-planned garden. An experienced gardener knows just what he wants to grow, and how long each plant needs to reach maturity. While watching the garden develop, he will let the healthy plants mature, and weed out the items that are not doing well. This is easy to do because there is little emotion involved on the gardener's part. Most investors have trouble executing this simple strategy because it is hard to admit when a mistake is made.

Comparing gardening to portfolio management yields some interesting results. Because of the inability to control their emotions and ego, many investors (and brokers) manage their securities exactly the opposite of the way a gardener tends his landscape. Assume an investor begins by purchasing five stocks. Three months later three of the stock prices are higher and two have gone lower. What does the insecure investor do? He sells the stocks that have had the highest returns and holds on to his losers. Imagine a gardener pulling out his healthiest plants while leaving the sick ones in the ground.

Why are portfolios mishandled? Many investors internalize their results, and their ego becomes their greatest enemy. The most unprofitable thought process works as follows: "If I take a profit, it proves that I made a good decision in the first place. Additionally, a loss is not a loss unless I sell." After several portfolio adjustments, this investor now finds himself paying capital gains taxes while holding on to a bunch of under-performing stocks. While this sounds ridiculous, it is exactly what many people do. If investors took the time to review past stocks in which they took profits, they will find that some of them have gone on to double and triple in price. It cannot be stressed enough—the key to successful investing is in taking small losses and letting your profits run.

Remember to use the Loeb Worksheet at the end of this chapter. It will assist you in creating a "ruling reason" for buying a stock. The effort required to complete this form elevates the knowledge needed to effectively execute a stock trading decision. By studying both the winning and losing stock transactions, and the reasons for their success or failure, your judgment as an investor will continue to improve. It is the ongoing self study and evaluation that will make you the best investor you can be.

Loeb Worksheet

Yale Hirsch, publisher of the annual *Stock Trader's Almanac,* has summarized the work of G.M. Loeb in the following pages. It includes a valuable worksheet called the "Investment Survival Checklist" to assist investors in making appropriate stock selections and maintain their discipline.

•••

G.M. LOEB'S "BATTLE PLAN" FOR INVESTMENT SURVIVAL

LIFE IS CHANGE: Nothing can ever be the same a minute from now as it was a minute ago. Everything you own is changing in price and value. You can find that last price of an active security on the stock ticker, but you cannot find the next price anywhere. The value of your money is changing. Even the value of your home is changing, though no one walks in front of it with a sandwich board consistently posting the changes.

RECOGNIZE CHANGE: Your basic objective should be to profit from change. The art of investing is being able to recognize change and to adjust investment goals accordingly.

WRITE THINGS DOWN: You will score more investment success and avoid more investment failures if you write things down. Very few investors have the drive and inclination to do this.

KEEP A CHECKLIST: If you aim to improve your investment results, try to get into the habit of keeping a checklist on every issue you consider buying. Before making a commitment, it will pay you to write down the answers to at least some of the basic questions—How much am I investing in this company? How much do I think I can make? How much do I have to risk? How long do I expect to take to reach my goal?

HAVE A SINGLE RULING REASON: Above all, writing things down is the best way to find "the ruling reason." When all is said and done, there is invariably a single reason that stands out above all others why a particular security transaction can be expected to show a profit. All too often many relatively unimportant statistics are allowed to obscure this single important point.

Any one of a dozen factors may be the point of a particular purchase or sale. It could be a technical reason—a coming increase in earnings or dividend not yet discounted in the market price—a change of management—a promising new product—an expected improvement in the market's valuation of earnings—or many others. But, in any given case, one of these factors will almost certainly be more important than all the rest put together.

CLOSING OUT A COMMITMENT: If you have a loss in your stocks, the solution is auto-matic, provided you decide what to do at the time you buy. Otherwise, the question divides itself into two parts. Are we in a bull or bear market? Few of us really know until it is too late. For the sake of the record, if you think it is a bear market, just put that consideration first and sell as much as your conviction suggests and your nature allows.

If you think it is a bull market, or at least a market where some stocks move up, some mark time and only a few decline, do not sell unless:

✔ You see a bear market ahead.

✔ You see trouble for a particular company in which you own shares.

✔ Time and circumstances have turned up a new and seemingly far better buy than the issue you like least in your list.

✔ Your shares stop going up and start going down.

A subsidiary question is, which stock to sell first? Two further observations may help here:

✔ Do not sell solely because you think a stock is "overvalued."

✔ If you want to sell some of your stocks and not all, in most cases it is better to go against your emotional inclinations and sell first the issues with losses, small profits or none at all, the weakest, the most disappointing, etc.

Mr. Loeb is the author of *The Battle for Investment Survival,* Fraser Publishing, Box 494, Burlington VT 05402.

G.M. LOEB'S INVESTMENT SURVIVAL checklist

Objectives and Risks

Security		Price	Shares	Date

"Ruling reason" for commitment	Amount of commitment
	$_____
	% of my investment capital
	_____%

Price objective	Est. time to achieve it	I will risk _____points	Which would be $_____

Technical Position

Price action of stocks:		Dow Jones Industrial Average
☐ hitting new highs	☐ in a trading range	
☐ pausing in an uptrend	☐ moving up from low ground	Trend of Market
☐ acting stronger than market	☐ _____	

Selected Yardsticks

	Price Range		Earnings Per Share Actual or Projected	Price/Earnings Ratio Actual or Projected
	High	Low		
Current Year				
Previous Year				

Merger Possibilities	Years for earnings to double in past
Comment on future	Years for market price to double in past

Periodic Re-checks

Date	Stock Price	D.J.I.A.	Comment	Action taken, if any

Completed Transactions

Date Closed	Period of time held	Profit or loss
Reason for profit or loss		

Courtesy of the Hirsch Organization

CHAPTER

12

Using Your
Home Computer

"Knowledge born from actual experience is the answer to why one profits;
lack of it is the reason one loses."
Gerald M. Loeb

There will always be individuals whose VCRs constantly blink 12:00AM. There are others who will never trust or use a bank's ATM machine. I am not a computer whiz, nor do you need to be in this age of "plug and play." In technological times like these, there are still a surprisingly high percentage of experienced and wealthy investors who are not using home computers to avail themselves of the myriad of available investment information.

Until a few years ago it was difficult to find financial data that would allow an investor to perform a detailed analysis of a company. Now, the current explosion of the Internet has made available a tremendous amount of information, and most of it is free. Many companies have their own website to obtain data. Investment software packages are available that compile and sort data on virtually all publicly traded companies. What is now available to individuals, used to be only accessible to the big financial institutions, and most often at prices prohibitive to all others.

The cost of setting up a home computer and purchasing an investment software package is within the financial reach of virtually all investors. I encourage you to plug into the information that is now within your grasp. I have been using a service for charts called Telescan™ (wallstreetcity.com). Fundamental data can be obtained through a number of excellent computer programs. There are other services available, just find the one that works best for you. I cannot teach you how to use a computer, but depending on the time you are willing to spend, your computer can become your main source of investment information. The proliferation of financial information now available on the Internet is truly amazing.

There are also a number of web-sites on the Internet that can be very helpful to investors. See the next chapter for an updated list.

13

Internet Sites for Investment Information

Listed below are some of the sites that I have bookmarked on my own computer. By no means is this a complete list, and more sites seem to become available almost daily.

INTERNET SITES FOR INVESTMENT INFORMATION

www.aaii.com

www.barrons.com

www.bloomberg.com

www.businessweek.com

www.cboe.com

www.cbsmarketwatch.com

www.cnnfn.com

www.cyberinvest.com

www.dailystocks.com

www.dorseywright.com

www.dowjones.com

www.earningswhispers.com

www.edgaronline.com

www.fool.com

www.go2net.com

www.hoovers.com

www.insidertrader.com

www.investools.com

www.investor.com

www.investorguide.com

www.investors.com

www.ipo.com

www.magnetinvesting.com

www.marketguide.com

www.moneyclub.com

www.morningstar.com

www.nasdaq.com

www.nyse.com

www.rcgonline.com

www.redherring.com

www.reuters.com

www.smartmoney.com

www.stockmaster.com

www.stockpoint.com

www.stocks.com

www.thewebinvestor.com

www.upside.com

www.wallstreetlinks.com

www.wallstreetcity.com

www.zacks.com

14

The MAGNET® Stock Selection Process

"Great spirits have always found violent opposition from mediocrities."
Albert Einstein

" It is a funny thing about life; if you refuse to accept
anything but the best, you very often get it."
W. Somerset Maugham

In the previous chapters, I have attempted to provide you with the prerequisites for successful investing. I have developed a relatively simple system to implement this plan that I would now like to share with you. It is called the MAGNET® Stock Selection Process, and in the past ten years this model has averaged over a 30% return per year. Appendix A contains a detailed backtesting of this ten-year study.

A MAGNET® stock contains a combination of technical and fundamental characteristics that pull investors into the shares, as though by magnetic attraction, resulting in a rapid price increase. I have studied hundreds of stocks during my investment career, and the top performers repeatedly display several common characteristics. In an effort to develop a workable system to select these stocks, dozens of fundamental indicators needed to be analyzed and backtested. The results of these efforts are a simple, clear and highly successful stock selection process that can used by all investors that have a computer.

The MAGNET® Stock Selection Process contains components of many theories that are covered in earlier chapters in this book, along with the best of fundamental and technical analysis. The simplest way to describe the system would be a combination of value, growth and momentum. The MAGNET® methodology encompasses the best of the momentum aspects of the market, while demanding the downside protection of a value approach, and insisting on top-line revenue growth. "MAGNET®" is an acronym that describes the characteristics of the companies that will "draw" investors towards them. The following is an outline of the elements contained in this acronym:

M: Management must be outstanding.
Momentum must be improving.

A: Acceleration of earnings, revenues and margins

G: Growth rate must exceed current valuation

N: New product or management may be the driver

E: Emerging industry or product creates great opportunity

T: Timing needs to be right
(Technically poised for large price increase)

Management and Momentum
Management

There is nothing more fundamentally important to a company than the capabilities of its management. Management must foster excellence, attract talented personnel, encourage employees to develop new products, deploy assets, market the company's product, and provide leadership.

Management ownership of a substantial percentage of its stock is also very important. It would be foolish for those executives with large stock holdings to act in a manner detrimental to the best interests of the company. Competitive salaries that include generous management bonuses tied to enhancing shareholder value are also important factors.

A discussion of management can be found in each company's 10K, quarterly, and annual reports to shareholders. Call the company's Investor Relations Department to obtain these documents.

Momentum

The momentum of a stock is the relationship of its share price to the overall market. This is commonly referred to as "relative strength", although many market technicians have created their own methods of computing and describing momentum. The easiest way to follow and track the momentum or relative strength of a company, without using your computer, is by reading the *Investor's Business Daily* newspaper, and it's weekly supplement, Daily Graphs. The relative strength line should be in an "up trend" for at least a few months. In fact, it is rare to lose on a stock whose relative strength line is hitting an annual high.

Acceleration of Earnings, Revenues and Margins

The acceleration of earnings, revenues, and margins are the central characteristics of a momentum growth company. There should be a minimum increase of 15% in quarterly revenues and earnings. This standard will elimi-nate most companies from consideration under the MAGNET® Stock Se-lection Process. In fact, many companies in which I have invested will be growing at a rate of 30% or better. The modest 15% is used in this model to avoid eliminating larger companies that may dominate their industries, but are simply too big to maintain the same rapid grow rate of a smaller company.

The gross profit margins are also an important consideration. While the profit margins need not be continually rising, they should not show a decline from prior reporting periods. If the profit margins begin to slip, something is amiss at the company. It is common in today's stock market for a company to report great earnings, only to see the stock's price decline dramatically. Often when profit margins are declining, the most aggressive and astute momentum investors are selling. They are anticipating a future earnings slowdown, telegraphing a loss in momentum.

Growth at a Discount

While individuals should own stocks in companies that maintain high growth rates, it is critical not to overpay for the stock based on its growth pros-pects. Ideally, when the stock is purchased, the current market valuation of a company, based on its P/E (price earnings ratio) should be one-half its growth rate. Therefore, if the company can reasonably grow at a projected 40% rate over the next several years, an investment in this stock should be made when the market temporarily assigns it a P/E of 20. This valuation normally occurs either before the company becomes "popular" with inves-tors, or when the stock is temporarily out of favor.

New Product or Management

When a stock enters into an increasing price momentum phase something new is usually occurring at the company. It may be new management that creates a change in direction or a new product is developed, creating a renewed awareness of the company.

New industries are spurred by new technologies, and these new companies are often growing the fastest. In today's momentum driven market, a stock hitting new highs will also gather new investors. A company's stock price tends to run up whenever something "new" catches the attention of investors.

Emerging Industry or Product

Companies in emerging industries represent some of the best investments. The dramatic advancements currently taking place in such fields as technology and medical science can result in extraordinary investment profits. Large gains can be made by experienced investors who possess a clear understanding of the future direction of technology, and/or the medical fields. Learn as much as you can about emerging industries.

Timing

Timing is critical to ensuring success in the stock market, as discussed in earlier chapters. Every investor must develop a method to answer the question, "When should I buy?" I incorporate several technical indicators that enhance timing, once a stock has met the fundamental requirements of the MAGNET® model discussed above. These include moving averages, stochastics, MACD (Moving Averages Converging Diverging), relative strength, volume analysis, insider trading, and Point & Figure charting.

Many charting programs combine all of these technical tools into one system. See Chapter 16 for a complete discussion. As stated earlier in our chapter on when to buy and sell, knowing when to buy a stock will greatly affect the profitability of the investment. One of the most disappointing results comes from buying stock in a great company at the wrong time, and not holding on. The result is the same as having made an investment in a sub par company—the investor loses money.

This is a summary of the MAGNET® Stock Selection Process. It is the culmination of the efforts of a team of professionals and many years of experience. We hope our work will help others achieve their financial goals.

15

Why the MAGNET® Stock Selection Process Works

"There is one thing stronger than all the armies in the world, and this is an idea whose time has come."

Victor Hugo

"Don't gamble! Take all savings and buy some good stock and hold it till it goes up, then sell it. If it don't go up, don't buy it."

Will Rogers

The MAGNET® Stock Selection Process has captured the attention of both individual and institutional investors. Not only does the process make sense, but the methodology has been implemented successfully in various applications.

- The MAGNET® "Simple" Search introduced in the first edition of *MAGNET® Investing* generated a one-year return of over 25%. The MAGNET® "Complex" Search returned over 90% during the same period.

- I employ the MAGNET® Stock Selection Process as the Market Strategist for First Montauk Securities Corp., which involves managing the Firm's "Focus List." The Focus List ranked number three among all monitored lists maintained by Zacks Investment Research in 1999.

- I manage a private fund utilizing the MAGNET® Stock Selection Process. Since the Fund's inception in 1997, it has outperformed the S&P 500 (220% vs. 79%), net of fees and expenses.

- The process has been licensed to a major mutual fund company and a major unit trust firm. Both companies engaged in their own due diligence and independent testing methodology.

All this has taken place in an environment in which approximately 60% of all stocks showed a decline in 1999. In fact, in the first edition of my book, I issued a warning not to pay too much attention to the major indexes, but instead to focus on stock selection. So why did the MAGNET® Stock Selection Process work so well in such a difficult investment environment?

In the simplest terms, our stock selection process produces a group of companies that will attract value, growth, and momentum investors alike. Our multi-disciplined approach pulls together the best from each field. Therefore, there is a much greater pool of buying power to push prices higher.

Another prominent feature that sets MAGNET® apart from other models is that the "growth" component is revenue based. This contrasts with the current investor focus on bottom line earnings. Over the last several years there has been a significant increase in "financial engineering." As many companies have experienced an inability to raise product prices, the focus has been on cost cutting, growth though mergers, and tricky one-time charges. Management cannot manipulate top line revenue growth. The MAGNET® system is not interested in companies reducing head-counts and taking special accounting charges, rather, we select companies that are adding staff and building new plants to keep up with growing demand for their new products.

MAGNET® only selects stocks that are priced at a discount to their internal growth rate. As of the writing of the 2nd edition, the market is undergoing a massive sell-off in the highest-flying stocks that have attracted pure momentum investors. These stocks were gobbled up by investors and day traders simply because of stories, strong price charts, and emotion. Once the trend turned negative, the holders of these companies became aggressive sellers, generating tremendously fast sell-offs. Months of steady gains were erased in days- sometimes hours. MAGNET® only selects stocks with significant underlying value.

While we are careful not to overpay for a company's growth, the MAGNET® Stock Selection Process does contain a momentum component that looks for stocks that are "under accumulation" by investors. Owning companies that have good fundamentals but are completely unrecognized by the market leave disappointed investors to mumble "but it is a good company." This was a mistake I made for years. Remember, the only reason to invest in the stock market is to make money.

Some investors were confused when they first reviewed the MAGNET® process. I am often asked, "Are there really any companies that meet the criteria of growth, value, and momentum analysis?" The reality is that there are very few, but our methodology has worked through several business and stock market cycles. Currently, out of almost 12,000 publicly traded companies, there are only about two hundred that meet the MAGNET® standards. Since most investors rarely own more twenty to thirty stocks, there are still plenty to chose from.

In conclusion, the system has withstood many professional tests, and worked in many live applications. I am confident that the MAGNET® Stock Selection Process will hold up to the test of time.

16

Performing a Search Using Your Computer

" Spend at least as much time researching a stock as
you would choosing a refrigerator."
Peter Lynch

" Luck is the preparation for, recognition of, and
proper seizure of opportunity."
Walter Heiby

In order to perform the search for MAGNET® stocks described in the preceding chapter, all you need is a computer, a modem, and a computerized search product that incorporates an online database of stocks that is continually updated. You can choose from a variety of products offered by Hoovers, Investools, Morningstar, Omega Research, Telescan, Worden Brother's, Zacks Research, etc.

Each of these products has tools (often called indicators) to screen their online databases. These tools can be used individually or combined to create thousands of different search strategies. Starting with a universe of stocks, the product can score and rank them, depending on your criteria. For example, if you ask for stocks with the lowest price/earnings ratio, the first stock on the list will have the lowest price/earnings ratio of all the stocks in the search universe. Many of the programs allow the user to select multiple indicators on any given search and find the stocks that best meet these combined goals.

Before we look at the MAGNET® Search, let's complete a simple but effective search that uses only one indicator. We are interested in finding stocks with high corporate insider buying, because this might signal an improvement in the company's business. Insiders are the officers, directors, and major shareholders who own more than ten-percent of a company's shares. We used Telescan's Prosearch™ in this example.

1. Select the indicator called "insider trading" and tell the computer to search the highest net insider buying.

2. Specify the number of stocks you want to see on the search report. We will ask for ten, but you could request as many as 250.

3. Select the universe of stocks you want to search. In this search we will use the entire available universe.

4. Submit the search to the online database. Save the search before you log on.

In a matter of seconds, the search will issue a report that ranks companies according to the number of insiders buying the stock. The more insiders buying, the higher the company will be ranked. Remember that your search results will vary from day to day and from service to service. With a few more keystrokes, you can also obtain additional data such as the names of those insiders buying stock, how many shares they bought, and the price they paid.

Adding more indicators, for example, the one-month change in consensus of Wall Street analyst's estimates, could further refine this search. We might also want to eliminate all stocks that sell below $5.00 (stock price indicator). Obviously, the results will change as additional indicators are added.

17

MAGNET®
Performance From
The First Edition
Of Our Book

"A trade that looks like it's designed by Stephen King has no more risk than one from Mr. Rogers. As long as you use an absolute dollar stop you will blast away the potential risk of what appears to be a risky trade."

"Always use stops."

Quotes from Larry Williams, author of
Long Term Secrets to Short Term Trading, and trading legend.

In the first edition of *MAGNET® Investing* we used our stock selection criteria and a software package called Telescan™ to create two model portfolios called MAGNET® "Simple" and MAGNET® "Complex." The twelve-month returns were 25.89% and 90.58%, respectively. Despite our screening and ranking process, there were a few stocks in our portfolios that had extremely poor returns. I point this out to restate the obvious; there is no process that only picks winners. I have included this chapter as a learning exercise and to demonstrate that every investor needs not only a workable stock selection methodology, but also proper portfolio management to achieve superior results.

Our large returns were generated in portfolios that had big losers. This is because while our screening process identifies a truly unique group of companies that are likely to be market leaders, circumstances often send stocks off course. An investor only needs a few winning stocks to make significant gains each year. The major indexes in 1999 posted impressive returns, including a remarkable 86% gain for the NASDAQ 100. However, again the advance /decline lines within the indexes showed continued deterioration. In fact, 60% of all stocks on the NYSE and NASDAQ finished lower for the year. In retrospect, our internal advance/ decline line was in great shape. (It is worth taking a moment to refer back to Chart 1-1 to further appreciate the importance of stock selection.)

Investors have the luxury to prune their portfolio, and control losses throughout the year, while the portfolio in our book was static. I looked back to the stocks in the portfolio that showed significant declines. In each case the story was slightly different- lower than expected revenue growth, key management defections, poor industry sector performance, and slowing profit margins were the general themes. Investors must periodically review each holding in an effort to eliminate the large losses that can develop through neglect. As discussed earlier, it is important to understand the risks of the stock market. Apparently good companies often end up making poor investments. Even after careful examination and study, unforeseen market forces can make the best analytical research look outright silly.

At the end of this chapter, we provide a few examples that show how using "stops" on long-term trend lines would have dramatically improved returns. By selling when a stock breaks its long-term trendline, catastrophic losses can be avoided. As we continue to update and re-score our MAGNET® portfolios, the companies that experience fundamental deterioration are naturally dropped off our radar screen. We recommend that investors buy current high ranked MAGNET® stocks, use stops, and let your profits run.

Here is a recap of the portfolios from the first edition of *MAGNET® Investing*.

MAGNET® Simple

	12/7/98	12/7/99	Point Change	Percentage Change	Comments
AEOS	28.56	45.38	16.81	58.86%	
AGPH	47.88	59.08	11.20	23.39%	No Longer Trades, Bought By WLA
CTAL	18.13	10.25	-7.88	-43.46%	
HAIN	18.06	23.25	5.19	28.74%	
JVLN	11.69	11.06	-0.63	-5.37%	
MCSC	24.69	38.94	14.25	57.71%	
NCI	41.75	10.75	-31.00	-74.25%	Formerly Metzler Group
PLCM	21.38	63.63	42.25	197.59%	
TAGS	33.13	9.50	-23.63	-71.33%	
THQI	19.92	37.25	17.33	87.04%	
TOTAL RETURN				25.89%	

MAGNET® Complex

	12/7/98	12/7/99	Point Change	Percentage Change	Comments
AEOS	28.56	45.38	16.81	58.86%	
NSOL	30.50	218.78	188.28	617.31%	
LSON	53.13	23.88	-29.25	-55.06%	
GPS	35.87	42.75	6.88	19.17%	
LIN	33.81	32.63	-1.19	-3.51%	
DELL	33.81	45.38	11.56	34.20%	
JKHY	52.50	45.88	-6.63	-12.62%	
ABDR	57.13	181.00	123.87	216.82%	No Longer Trades, Bought By DCLK
NCOG	38.75	34.31	-4.44	-11.45%	
INSS	35.42	50.31	14.89	42.04%	No Longer Trades, Bought By LU
TOTAL RETURN				90.58%	

Chart 17-1

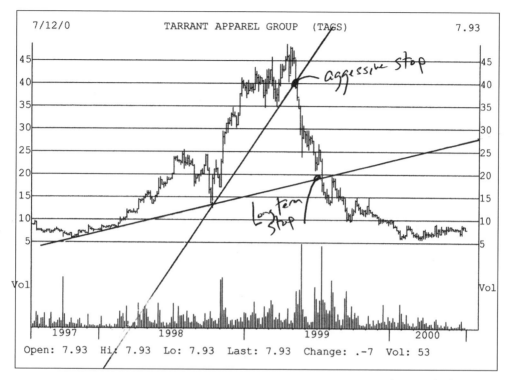

Courtesy of Telescan, Inc.

Depending on how aggressive you trade and which trendline you use, you would have cut your losses on Tarrant Apparel.

Chart 17-2

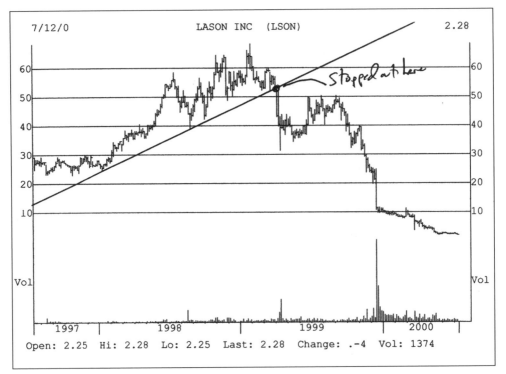

Courtesy of Telescan, Inc.

Using trendlines and stops, Lason would have been sold early in 1999 with almost no loss.

18

Searching
for
MAGNET® Stocks

*"Get inside information from the President and you will probably
lose half your money. If you get it from the Chairman of the Board,
you will lose all of your money."*

Jim Rogers

This chapter contains two search results through which we were seeking
current and future MAGNET® stocks as of mid-2000. Search #1 (MAGNET®
Simple) represents a simplified version of the quantifiable core (the "MAG")
of the MAGNET® Stock Selection Process (momentum, accelerating revenue growth, and growth ratio). The search performed in the first edition
of *MAGNET® Investing* returned over 25%. It allows even the novice investor to capture a significant portion of the returns we were able to generate

in our mathematically backtested study described in Appendix A. The second search, Search #2, (MAGNET® Complex) adds several additional filters that assist us in quantifying the more subjective "NET" (new, emerging, timing) of our MAGNET® process. It also allows the more experienced investor to draw on his own preferences in selecting stocks.

The search for new MAGNET® stocks requires the use of several indicators to identify future stock market leaders. Let's identify the fundamental criteria.

Search #1 (MAGNET® Simple) - The Core of the MAGNET® Stock Selection Process

The searches in this chapter were performed using Telescan™ Prosearch™. The first step in our search is to make sure to select stocks that are trading with positive momentum, since many great companies are not recognized by the market. However, once momentum is created, more and more money flows into these stocks. This is measured by a stock's "relative strength." We set the parameters to those stocks whose relative strength both over the last twelve weeks and the last fifty-two weeks is "relatively high." This step establishes a universe of stocks with momentum. We opened our search to our entire database of over 15,000 stocks, but this first search cuts our universe significantly.

In our second step, we are seeking companies that are growing faster than others in the same industry. You might think that net earnings would provide this information, but this indicator can be misleading since there are all types of accounting methods and one-time charges for events. One indicator that cannot be misrepresented is revenue growth. Therefore our second screening criteria is that revenue growth must be greater than 15%. At this stage, we now have a universe of stocks trading with momentum and strong revenue growth, but there is one more step we must complete in this search. Note that our universe of available stocks is once again cut significantly.

The last indicator is going to show stocks that meet the criteria of "growth at a discount." Each program has its own measurement for what is now commonly referred to as "G.A.R.P." Growth ratio compares a company's annualized five-year projected earnings per share (EPS) growth rate to its projected price/earnings (P/E) ratio for the next fiscal year. We want to identify stocks whose growth ratio is "relatively high," because this eliminates those stocks that are currently "over loved" and "over valued" by the market, and therefore do not offer growth at a discount.

At this point in the search, the "core" (relative strength, strong revenue growth, and growth ratio) of the MAGNET® Stock Selection Process has been implemented.

We are now ready to run the search. We have our parameters set to select two hundred stocks and then run them on three-year charts. In our first technical evaluation, we want to see the long-term picture and focus on short-term charts later.

Search 1

Criteria	Criteria Values
COMPANY GROWTH RATIO	High 100%
SALES GROWTH 1-YR	15.0-999998.0 a
RELATIVE PERFORMANCE	12-WK High 100%
RELATIVE PERFORMANCE	1-YR High 100%

(Telescan™ search)

Our "top ten" favorites of the two hundred stocks are listed here. This "top ten" required additional homework, including use of our own internal model and a proprietary MAGNET® scoring system.

COMPANY	TICKER	Growth Ratio	Sales Growth	Percentage Change in Price 12 Wks Relative to S&P 500	Percentage Change in Price 52 Weeks
Asyst Technologies, Inc.	ASYT	154.01	167.92	5.71	363.23
Vintage Petroleum, Inc.	VPI	245.20	424.05	52.25	95.65
Nvidia Corporation	NVDA	533.37	136.67	12.13	343.06
Xeta Technologies, Inc.	XETA	32.83	85.00	-6.47	258.62
Berry Petroleum Company "A"	BRY	685.76	121.06	-1.77	21.64
Imperial Oil Limited	IMO	111.63	43.24	30.45	35.05
1-800 Contacts, Inc.	CTAC	186.59	50.02	0.11	35.97
Flextronics International, Ltd.	FLEX	24.71	147.67	-4.71	96.77
AVX Corporation	AVX	236.86	30.90	38.51	310.18
California Amplifier, Inc.	CAMP	354.62	130.55	-42.60	497.10

Telescan™ charts and Market Guide fundamental data for each of these ten stocks can be found in Appendix B.

This unique and powerful combination of tools has generated an excellent starting point in the process of discovering the truly best stock opportunities. As you become more experienced and knowledgeable, more filters can be applied to identify additional stocks that will generate superior returns.

Search #2 (MAGNET® Complex)- A More detailed Search

This search picks up where the first ended by incorporating many other indicators that our stock selection system evaluates. They include additional filters such as stock price above eight, relative P/E ratio, price to sales ratio, earnings growth and debt to equity. In our first edition, this search returned over 90% in twelve months.

The second search was performed to uncover only the most powerful stocks from our universe. In fact, only thirty-two stocks met our criteria, even though we had requested two hundred. It gives you an idea of the unique combination of screens that can be used to create your own model.

Depending on market conditions, the economy, and a continuous testing of the factors that are generating current relative strength, we may incorporate additional "screens" or indicators. You can develop a personal search that incorporates your own criteria.

Search 2

Criteria	Criteria Values
STOCK PRICE	8.0-999998.0 a
MARKET CAPITALIZATION	1.0-999998.0 a
PERCENTAGE OF INSTITUTIONAL HOLDINGS	Low 80%
CURRENT RATIO	1.5-999998.0 a
DEBT/EQUITY RATIO	-99998.0-40.0 a
RELATIVE P/E RATIO	Low 100%
PRICE/SALES RATIO	Low 100%
LST-SQR DEVIATIONN 3-YR	Low 100%
COMPANY/INDUSTRY GROWTH RATIO	High 100%
COMPANY/S&P GROWTH RATIO	High 100%
PRICE RANK	85.0-999998.0 a
EPS RANK	80.0-999998.0 a
ACCUMULATION/DISTRIBUTION	High 100%
ERG	High 100%
ERG CHANGE 3-WK	High 100%
RELATIVE PERFORMANCE	6-WK 75.0-999998.0 a
RELATIVE PERFORMANCE	1-YR 75.0-999998.0 a
SALES GROWTH	1-YR 25.0-999998.0 a
EARNINGS GROWTH 1-YR	High 100%

(Telescan™ search)

The results of the second search, uncovering only thirty-two stocks, can be found in Appendix B.

Here is the list of the top ten stocks we selected after completing our final review and evaluation.

COMPANY	TICKER	Growth Ratio	Sales Growth	Percentage Change in Price 12 Wks Relative to S&P 500	Percentage Change in Price 52 Weeks
Flextronics International, Ltd.	FLEX	24.71	147.67	-4.71	96.77
TRC Companies, Inc.	TRR	71.56	32.03	-2.52	126.92
Kemet Corporation	KEM	807.44	45.36	32.41	473.2
Topps Company, Inc.	TOPP	310.30	63.11	25.76	53.23
Three-Five Systems	TFS	874.06	64.16	103.31	856.04
TTI Telecom International, Ltd.	TTIL	18.59	61.57	-26.73	225.58
M-Systems, Inc.	FLSH	-32.20	134.85	15.45	1276.47
Cybex Computer Products Corp.	CBXC	26.75	46.53	-14.60	99.44
Black Box Corporation	BBOX	0.78	52.47	3.85	70.88
Logitech International SA ADR	LOGIY	17.31	35.91	0.53	319.17

Telescan™ charts and Market Guide fundamental data for each of these ten stocks can be found in Appendix B.

The two searches described in this chapter are merely samples of the almost infinite combinations of variables that can be analyzed to uncover stock ideas. You can experiment and continue to refine your searches as your confidence develops.

In making stock selection decisions for Magnet, I first run my search as described in the preceding chapters. I then turn to a fundamental program and look at the following indicators, both individually and in comparison to their industry group: cash flow per share, return on equity, price to cash flow, sales growth, P/E, price to sales, price to book, twelve-month vs.

five-year trailing sales, operating and gross margins, revenue and net income per employee.

By tracking the best performing sectors and companies, and then ranking them in a value-oriented system, I am able to generate a list of outstanding companies and stock ideas. These "MAGNETS" should continue to attract more attention and provide excellent investment returns. However, because of ever-changing market conditions and specific events within companies, these lists are not being provided as recommendations to purchase these stocks. Rather, we have walked you through this selection process to show how empowering this system can be.

19

Maximizing Tax Efficiency Using the MAGNET® Stock Selection Process

" Always sell what shows you a loss and keep what shows you profit. "
Jesse Livermore

Excessive portfolio turnover is not tax efficient, and a balance must be struck between overactive trading (capital gains) and an under-performing portfolio. To achieve your long-term financial goals you need to consider the after-tax returns that you are generating.

In our application of the MAGNET® Stock Selection Process, the question of "persistence of returns" comes into play. That is, how long can a company's stock continue to perform exceptionally well? A company will often achieve a high rank using our system, but only for a short period of time. If you fall in love with a company, or stubbornly stick with poor performing stocks, your returns will suffer. On the other hand, you might believe that your returns would lag behind those investors holding on for the real big moves if you trade. We can show why it is better to stay invested in stocks that currently rank high under the MAGNET® system and rebalance relatively frequently, even after tax considerations.

A company's rank will change because of its earnings releases and the relative strength of its stock price. Therefore, it is important to maintain current "best ideas" in your portfolio. As an example, the following chart shows that quarterly rebalancing of the portfolio yielded an annualized return of 32.5%. When the portfolio was rebalanced annually, the return fell to a still impressive 22.4%.

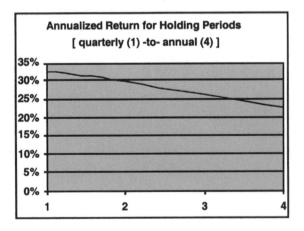

The reason for this decline is quite simple. Each quarter, publicly traded companies report earnings and other financial data to the Securities and Exchange Commission (SEC). This information is stored electronically and becomes immediately available for download by all investors, and the major financial data providers enter this information into their databases for distribution worldwide. Consequently, each quarter Magnet Investment Group can access new databases to analyze and rank using our stock selection process. In practice, about half of our portfolio turns over each quarter, while the other half continues to be held through the next quarter.

We also need to ask whether tax considerations should determine MAGNET® stock holding periods, notwithstanding the decline in returns for longer holding periods shown above. Capital gains for stock held less than a year are currently taxed as ordinary income (up to 39.6% maximum tax bracket) whereas stocks held longer are taxed at the lower capital gains rate (20%). This could make a difference in how we manage our MAGNET® portfolios. In practice, faster MAGNET® turnover yields higher returns.

In the following table we combine the annualized returns for MAG-NET® stock portfolios with tax implications. For example, we see in the first line that quarterly rebalancing yields a portfolio return of 32.5%. An investor in the maximum income tax bracket of 39.6% would show an after-tax return of 19.6%. The second line shows that the same investor would have an after tax return of 17.9% if the MAGNET® stocks were held for the full year. For investors in lower tax brackets, quarterly rebalancing becomes even more favorable.

Table 19-1. Tax Implications

Rebalance	Annualized Return	Tax bracket	Net after tax	Tax bracket	Net after tax
Quarter	32.5%	39.6%	19.6%	28.0%	23.4%
Annual	22.4%	20%	17.9%	20%	17.9%

In practice, there are two issues that reinforce the MAGNET® approach of frequent rebalancing. First, in Table 19-1 above we assume complete turnover of the portfolio within the year. Depending on market conditions, there are some periods when turnover is less than one hundred percent annually, and the return to investors would actually be a bit above the estimates in table 19-1.

Second, and more significant, is the number of fundamental variables that are included in the MAGNET® Stock Selection Process. The analysis above is based upon the MAGNET® "Simple" approach, however, in practice, the MAGNET® "Complex" strategy uses additional variables. As more variables are added to the system, there are increasing opportunities for any one of them to change, thus altering the rank of any given MAGNET® stock, and trading must respond to these changes in ranking. The resulting benefit of using the "Complex" strategy and rebalancing as necessary, is an annualized return that is about double that of the MAGNET® "Simple" strategy.

In conclusion, our quantitative model that assesses ideal holding periods tells us that "persistence of returns" depends on the number of indicators or screens that are employed. The larger the number, the shorter the holding period. But remember the screening process will identify the handful of true MAGNET® stocks that will continue to rank high over a multi-year period and make a marked difference in an investor's portfolio returns.

In essence, we would prefer to pay taxes than to sit on poor investments.

20

Recommended Reading

*"The man who does not read good books
has no advantage over the man who can't read them."*
Mark Twain

*"If all the economists in the world were laid end to end,
they still wouldn't reach a conclusion."*
George Bernard Shaw

I have read several dozen books on investing, and have tried to incorporate the best ideas, and experiment with different techniques. Many lessons have been learned through trial and error, but it has all finally come together in the MAGNET® Stock Selection Process. While MAGNET® can work for others, my knowledge and experience cannot be fully transferred in this book. It is important for those who are determined to invest profitably, to spend the time reading throughout their investment career.

Here is an updated list of some of the books that I have read and feel would be helpful to other investors. The books I consider the most beneficial and insightful are in *italics*.

TITLE (in alphabetical order)	AUTHOR(S)
Al Frank's New Prudent Speculator	Al Frank
The Battle for Investment Survival	Gerald M. Loeb
The Book of Investing Wisdom	Peter Krass
Beating the Dow	John Downes, Michael B. O'Higgins
Beating the Street	Peter Lynch
Being Right or Making Money	Ned Davis
Beyond Candlesticks	Steve Nison
Beyond Greed and Fear	Hersh Shefrin
Blood in the Streets	James Dale Davidson & Sir William Rees-Mog
Blue Chips & Hot Tips	W. Keith Schilit & Howard M. Schilit
Common Stocks and Uncommon Profits	Philip A. Fisher
Contrary Investing for the 90's	Richard E. Band
The Craft of Investing	John Train
Cyber Investing	David L. Brown & Kassandra Bentley
Extraordinary Popular Delusions and the Madness of Crowds	Charles Mackay
The Great Boom Ahead	Harry S. Dent, Jr.
The Handbook of Fixed Income Investing	Frank J. Fabozzi
How I Made $2,000,000 in the Stock Market	Nicolas Darvas
How to Buy Stocks	Louis Engel
How to Make Money in Stocks	William J. O'Neil
How to Trade in Stocks	Jesse Livermore
The Innergame of Investing	Derrick Niederman
The Innergame of Trading	Robert Koppel & Howard Abel
The Intelligent Investor	Benjamin Graham
Invest Like the Best	James P. O'Shaughnessy
Investment Biker: On the Road With Jim Rogers	Jim Rogers
Investment Gurus	Peter J. Tanous
Investment Policy	Charles D. Ellis
An Investor's Anthology	Charles D. Ellis
Long Term Secrets to Short Term Trading	Larry Williams
Market Wizards	Jack D. Schwager
Martin Zweig's Winning on Wall Street	Martin Zweig
Methods of a Wall Street Master	Victor Sperandeo
The Money Game	Adam Smith
The Money Masters	John Train
The New Market Wizards	Jack D. Schwager
The New Money Masters	John Train
The 100 Best Stocks to Own in America	Gene Walden

One Up on Wall Street	Peter Lynch
Peak Performers	Charles Garfield
Pennies on the Dollar	Gray Emerson Cardiff
The Plungers and the Peacocks	Dana L. Thomas
Point & Figure Charting	Thomas J. Dorsey
Point and Figure Construction and Formation	Michael Burke
The Prudent Investor	Al Frank
The Psychology of Investing	Lawrence E. Lifson &Richard A. Geist
A Random Walk down Wall Street	Burton G. Malkiel
Reminiscences of a Stock Operator	Edwin Lefvere
The Science of Making Money in Precious Metals	Gray Emerson Cardiff
Secrets for Profiting in Bull and Bear Markets	Stan Weinstein
Sector Rotation	Sam Stovall
Stock Market Rules	Michael D. Sheimo
Stock Traders Almanac (annually)	Yale Hirsch
Super Stocks	Kenneth L. Fisher
The Super Traders	Alan Rubenfeld
Trader Vic	Victor Sperandeo
Trading for a Living	Dr. Alexander Elder
Trading Rules	William F. Eng
Trading to Win	Ari Kiev, MD
Truth of the Stock Tape	William D. Gann
The Warren Buffett Way	Robert G. Hagstrom, Jr.
What Works on Wall Street	James P. O' Shaughnessy
When To Sell	Justin & Robert Mamis

21

Putting it all Together

"The quality of a person's life is in direct proportion to their commitment to excellence, regardless of their chosen field of endeavor. "
Vince Lombardi

"A good trader has to have three things: a chronic inability to accept things at face value, to feel continuously unsettled, and to have humility."
Michael Steinhardt

I have covered quite a bit of ground in this book. Investing is a combination of science and psychology, and as such, each investor must understand his "emotional chemistry" and tailor an investment strategy around it. The importance of proper stock selection has been highlighted and the MAGNET® Stock Selection Process has been introduced. I used a case study and guided you through the powerful tools of Telescan™'s ProSearch™ in an attempt to identify potential great stocks. The challenge is to use all this information in a manner that works for you.

There is an ongoing debate within the investment community. One side "trades for profits" and the other "buys and holds." The MAGNET® Stock Selection Process incorporates both. Again, it is going to be up to you to combine the two in a manner in which you are most comfortable. Buying and holding the "wrong" stocks is a sure-fire ticket to the poor house. Taking small profits in companies that turn into major winners can feel equally frustrating. Try the "gardening approach" described earlier in this book. It allows an investor to be patient and let his winners grow, while periodically weeding out those ideas that simply are not developing.

In Appendix A, Dr. T. Owen Carroll provides a ten-year backtesting of the MAGNET® Stock Selection Process. It has averaged an annual return in excess of 30% per year over the past ten years. In this system, a quarterly re-balancing of the entire portfolio is conducted. In other words, the top ranked stocks comprise the portfolio, and the same analysis is conducted again at the beginning of the following quarter. The portfolio is then adjusted to incorporate the new top ranked stocks. This system completely eliminates emotion and has produced returns that could create enormous wealth, despite the tax implications of high portfolio turnover. Appendix B contains the results of the MAGNET® Simple and MAGNET® Complex searches performed in Chapter 18. We provide a Telescan™ chart and a Market Guide "Quick Facts" summary for each of the top ten stocks selected by our final MAGNET® analysis.

Throughout my career, many individual stock trades and recommendations have helped define my investment style. I have reviewed my old files and retrieved the original charts and comments. Appendix C provides several examples of individual trades that helped me develop the MAGNET® Stock Selection Process.

I hope this book provides the foundation for you to accept the challenge of superior investing and creates the momentum to help you improve your investment returns. I encourage you to use Chapter 20 to select a few books to read that will further your interest and knowledge. Set your goals high and do not let any of the inevitable setbacks derail you. It is time to get started. . . best of luck and healthy profits ahead.

A

Testing The MAGNET® Approach

The MAGNET® approach to the stock market is intended to provide robust growth combined with substantial value in it's stock selections. This timely investment approach uses research and analysis of fundamental financial data for corporations to identify strong, competitive companies versus weak companies. The difference in stock price appreciation between the two extremes is so profound that we can "buy the best and avoid the rest." Even under difficult conditions in the equity markets, the profit spread of the MAGNET® strategy versus, say, the S&P 500 index remains near double digits annually in our research over the last ten years. We tested the core of the MAGNET® strategy against the S&P 500 index as shown in the chart on the next page.

Chart A-1

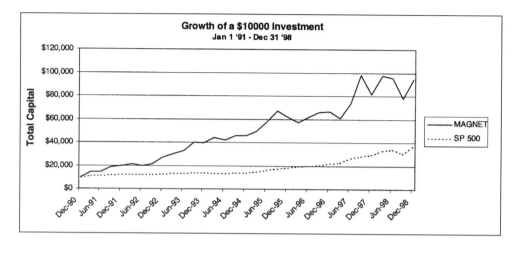

	MAGNET®	S&P 500
Average annual return	32.5%	17.8%
Sharpe ratio (annualized)	2.07	1.84

MAGNET® CORE STOCK SELECTION

As described in Chapter 18, MAGNET® is founded on a computer-based analysis of cash flow for and into companies. In contrast to a simple free cash flow or earnings forecast, the MAGNET® cash flow analysis integrates relative strength, sales (revenue), and growth ratio to determine when a company's stock is expected to become stronger or weaker.

The MAGNET® Stock Selection Process enables us to observe critical changes in the fundamentals of a company ahead of other market observers and to focus specifically on a company's increasing strength or its growing weakness.

Computer-based analysis of corporate data is employed to assure a consistent application of our MAGNET® Stock Selection Process and to obtain reduced risk portfolios. In practice, before trading, stocks are then reviewed individually for recent and/or new information that might not be available to the computer-based screening process. Stocks may be eliminated from consideration based on such a review, but a stock is never added into the portfolio unless it satisfies the computer implemented selection criteria described in Chapter 14.

HISTORICAL UNIVERSE

For testing the MAGNET® approach, we used the Compustat database of quarterly fundamentals and prices for the last ten years. From this universe, we selected 2000 stocks with the greatest sales at each end-of-quarter in the last ten years. Sales is a far more appropriate standard to select stable companies with liquidity than market capitalization. Indeed, some technology stocks have high market capitalization and no sales, hardly the kind of stocks we seek for a strategy intended to consistently show wealth growth in the coming market. After cleaning the database for errors and missing corporate information, we were generally left with 1500 or more stocks in the universe. Stocks with high rankings on sales, earnings and price behavior are selected for the long side positions in the portfolio.

MAGNET® analysis is summarized in a ranking of the cash flow growth measures for each stock in the universe.

BUILDING THE CORE OF THE MAGNET® APPROACH

The universe of stocks described above had an average annualized return of 15.9% over the eight-year backtesting horizon. For each of the elements of MAGNET®, the contribution to an excess return over the index of all stocks is shown in the table below.

Index of the universe	15.9%
Growth in sales	17.4%
Growth in earnings	18.6%
Price-to-earnings ratio	17.6%
Relative strength	24.1%
MAGNET® (combined rank)	32.5%

In practice, we divided stocks in the universe into seven ranks, from -3 to +3. The eight-year average annualized returns for each rank are shown in the chart below. You will notice the discrimination between top and bottom ranked stocks exceeds 20% annually.

Chart A-2

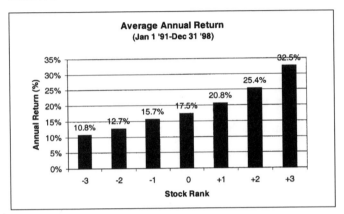

The cumulative returns of MAGNET® top-ranked and bottom-ranked stocks (the upper and lower lines below) and of the universe of more than a thousand stocks for which sufficient data was available in the Compustat database and the S&P 500 Index (the dotted line) are shown in Chart A-3 below.

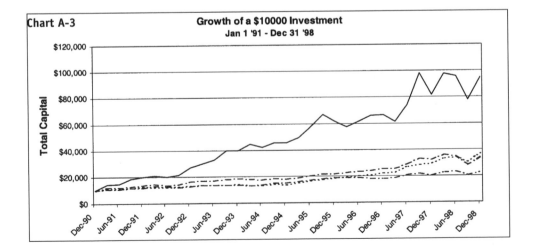

	TOP RANK	BOTTOM RANK	UNIVERSE	S&P500
Average annual return	32.5%	10.8%	15.9%	17.8%
Sharpe ratio (annualized)	2.07	1.03	1.61	1.84

Below were the quarterly returns in both graph and table format.

Chart A-4

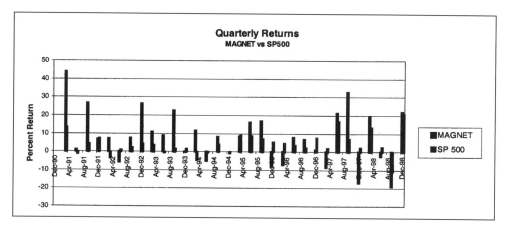

QTR ENDING	RANK +3	RANK -3	SP 500
Dec-90			
Mar-91	43.9	9.4	13.6
Jun-91	1.0	1.6	-1.1
Sep-91	26.9	6.0	4.5
Dec-91	6.8	2.6	7.5
Mar-92	7.0	10.8	-3.2
Jun-92	-5.7	-5.7	1.1
Sep-92	7.4	-2.2	2.4
Dec-92	26.3	3.7	4.3
Mar-93	10.8	8.2	3.7
Jun-93	8.9	0.4	-0.3
Sep-93	22.5	0.3	1.9
Dec-93	-0.4	-0.8	1.6
Mar-94	11.6	-2.7	-4.4
Jun-94	-4.9	1.9	-0.3
Sep-94	8.0	9.8	4.1
Dec-94	-0.1	-0.7	-0.7
Mar-95	8.6	7.3	9.0
Jun-95	16.1	6.4	8.8
Sep-95	16.8	5.5	7.3
Dec-95	-8.0	4.4	5.4
Mar-96	-7.1	0.0	4.8
Jun-96	7.8	2.0	3.9

continued

QTR ENDING	RANK +3	RANK -3	SP 500
Sep-96	6.6	-6.8	2.5
Dec-96	1.1	1.9	7.8
Mar-97	-8.3	0.9	2.2
Jun-97	21.3	12.9	16.9
Sep-97	32.9	5.0	7.0
Dec-97	-16.9	-7.3	2.4
Mar-98	19.6	13.6	13.5
Jun-98	-2.2	0.6	2.9
Sep-98	-18.7	-11.6	-10.9
Dec-98	21.9	11.5	20.9
Mean	8.2%	2.8%	4.3%
Sigma	14.2%	6.0%	6.2%
Info ratio	0.58	0.46	0.70

PRACTICAL INSIGHTS INTO THE MAGNET® APPROACH

In practice, price trends over the past year were examined to determine whether strong or improving fundamentals had been priced into each stock. In addition, price-to-sales and price-to-gross cash flow ratios were used as measures of price relative to fundamentals. MAGNET® analysis was summarized in a ranking on the cash flow growth measures for each stock in the universe. We then employed straightforward pattern recognition technology to identify specific behaviors of the MAGNET® stock selection criteria required for future price appreciation. This methodology is embedded in the rigorous computer-based Stock Selection Process.

Quarterly re-balancing was done as new fundamental data became available for stocks. The updated fundamental data for all stocks in the portfolio was passed through our computer processing. Stocks that no longer met the MAGNET® stock selection criteria were removed from the portfolio as we re-deployed capital to stocks with higher possibilities for price appreciation.

Following, are the results of each quarterly MAGNET® selection for the last year of our test (1998).

1st Quarter Symbol	1998 Open	Close	Return
BAANF	33.00	47.88	45.09
BY	22.88	25.88	13.11
CBR	58.00	69.94	20.59
CCE	35.56	36.69	3.18
CNS	43.94	42.94	-2.28
CPWR	32.00	49.38	54.31
DELL	84.00	135.52	61.33
DLJ	79.50	84.88	6.77
DO	48.13	45.38	-5.71
GECM	11.50	12.13	5.48
JEF	40.94	56.50	38.01
MAM	21.75	28.69	31.91
MER	72.94	83.00	13.79
MRLL	23.25	22.00	-5.38
ORB	29.75	44.88	50.86
SCR.A	32.00	38.56	20.50
VOL	53.88	55.75	3.47
VRC	21.44	25.75	20.10
VTS	39.50	50.56	28.00
WFT	51.75	46.31	-10.51
Avg.	41.79	50.13	19.63

2nd Quarter Symbol	1998 Open	Close	Return
ATI	48.94	58.44	19.41
BY	25.88	21.50	-16.92
CBR	69.94	76.00	8.66
CELL	17.19	14.50	-15.65
CPWR	49.38	51.13	3.54
DELL	67.75	92.81	36.98
DLJ	84.88	101.62	19.72
GDT	73.37	71.31	-2.81
GECM	12.13	4.63	-61.83
JEF	56.50	41.00	-27.43
KOF	20.44	17.38	-14.97
MPS	34.50	31.25	-9.42
MWL	37.88	43.38	14.52
NFB	38.37	36.66	-4.46
RCOT	26.25	33.50	27.62
RJF	43.56	44.91	3.10
SCR.A	38.56	38.25	-0.80
TNL	39.19	39.94	1.91
VRC	25.75	19.81	-23.07
VTS	50.56	49.94	-1.23
Avg.	43.05	44.40	-2.16

3rd Quarter Symbol	1998 Open	Close	Return
ATI	58.44	57.00	-2.46
CBR	38.00	20.13	-47.03
CCE	39.13	25.25	-35.47
CDN	31.25	25.56	-18.21
CPWR	51.13	58.88	15.16
CTL	45.88	47.25	2.99
CUI	45.63	24.69	-45.89
DELL	92.81	131.49	41.67
DLJ	50.81	25.56	-49.69
GDT	71.31	74.25	4.12
HHS	25.81	22.38	-13.29
KEA	56.00	36.00	-35.71
MCK	81.50	91.63	12.43
MCY	64.44	37.50	-41.81
MLT	13.69	8.38	-38.79
NLCS	24.00	29.50	22.92
OTRKB	25.00	25.00	0.00
RCOT	33.50	19.50	-41.79
TWMC	43.13	27.38	-36.52
VTS	49.94	16.69	-66.58
Avg.	47.07	40.20	-18.70

4th Quarter Symbol	1998 Open	Close	Return
ADMS	17.44	19.25	10.38
ATI	57.00	72.66	27.47
BMCS	60.06	44.56	-25.80
CPWR	58.88	78.13	32.69
CTL	47.25	67.50	42.86
ENE	53.50	57.06	6.65
GDT	74.25	110.25	48.48
GPS	35.13	56.13	59.78
GVA	29.44	33.56	14.00
MCCO	16.84	26.50	57.36
MCK	91.63	79.06	-13.72
MYG	47.75	62.25	30.37
NLCS	29.50	37.00	25.42
OTRKB	25.00	33.13	32.52
PMS	40.50	50.50	24.69
RAD	35.50	45.56	28.35
RCOT	19.50	17.94	-8.01
SDS	31.50	39.69	25.99
SIG	32.31	35.75	10.65
TWMC	18.25	19.69	7.88
Avg.	42.36	49.31	21.90

B

ProSearch Results from Chapter 18

Telescan Charts and Market Guide "Quick facts"
for Search 1 (MAGNET® Simple) "Top Ten" Stocks

CHART B-1

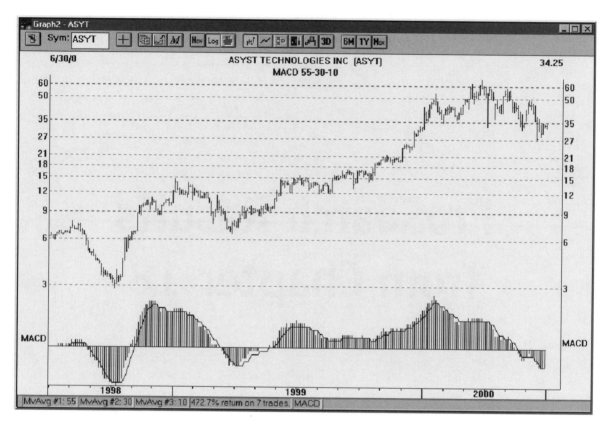

Asyst Technologies, Inc. current 2 year

Quick Facts
QKFACT ASYT   04648X107 Asyst Technologies, Inc.

Market Guide Quick Facts Report

Asyst Technologies, Inc.	SYMBOL: ASYT	EXCHANGE:	NASD

PRICING DATA (AS OF)	07/14/00	RATIOS & STATISTICS	
Price	36.50	Price/Revenue (TTM)	4.81
52 Week High	67.00	P/E (TTM)	160.79
52 Week Low	11.91	Price/Book (MRQ)	5.00
Beta	2.76	Price/Cash Flow (TTM)	59.06
Avg Daily Vol (10 Day)	0.91 Mil	ROA (TTM)	5.17%
Avg Daily Vol (3 Month)	0.81 Mil	ROE (TTM)	6.58%
		Current Ratio (MRQ)	2.82
DIVIDEND INFORMATION		Total Debt/Equity (MRQ)	0.12
Indicated Annual ($)	0.00		
Yield	0.00%	NOTE: TTM = trailing twelve months	
		MRQ = most recent quarter	

SHARE RELATED INFORMATION		SHORT INTEREST INFORMATION	
Market Cap. ($)	1,190.521 Mil	Current Month	0.277 Mil
Shares Out.	32.617 Mil	Previous Month	0.392 Mil
Float	28.400 Mil	Short Interest Ratio	0.5 Day

INSTITUTIONAL & INSIDER OWNERSHIP

	PURCHASES	SALES	NET PURCH	%OWNED
Institutions (3 Months)	7.972 Mil	7.245 Mil	0.726 Mil	76.7%
Insiders (6 Months)	0.000 Mil	0.598 Mil	-0.598 Mil	12.9%

BUSINESS SUMMARY
ASYT develops, manufactures and markets systems
utilizing isolation technology, material tracking products &
factory automation solutions used in cleanrooms for
semiconductor manufacturing. For the FY ended 3/31/00,
revenues totaled $225.6M, up from $92.9M. Net income
totaled $10M vs. a loss of $26.9M. Results reflect increased
demand for the company's products and higher international
sales. Earnings also reflect material cost reductions.

REVENUES (Thousands of U.S. Dollars)

QUARTERS	1997	1998	1999	2000
JUN	33,148	37,686	37,441	27,086
SEP	33,085	40,312	18,900	40,696
DEC	36,432	42,310	17,911	63,816
MAR	34,855	45,155	18,696	93,956
TOTAL	137,520	165,463	92,948	225,554

EARNINGS PER SHARE

	1997	1998	1999	2000
JUN	0.170	0.150	0.040	-0.120
SEP	0.165	0.185	-0.600	-0.110
DEC	0.080	0.205	-0.270	0.180
MAR	0.130	0.210	-0.320	0.270
TOTAL	0.545	0.750	-1.150	0.220

FY'98 Q's are restated for acquisitions.   FY'98-'00 fncls.
are and FY'99 Q's are being restated for the 8/99
acquisition of Palo Alto Technologies, Inc.

GROWTH RATES	1 YEAR	3 YEAR	5 YEAR
Revenue	142.67%	17.93%	45.21%
EPS	NM%	-15.90%	6.48%
Dividend	NM%	NM%	NM%

(Load Date: 7/17/00)
Database: Quick Facts
Keyword(s): (ASYT)

End of Report

CHART B-2

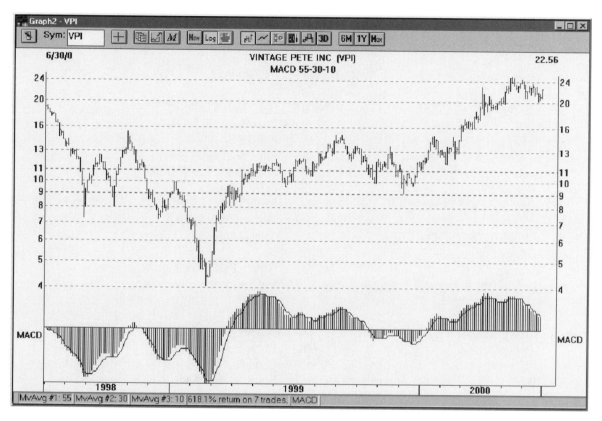

Courtesy of Telescan, Inc.

Vintage Petroleum, Inc. current 2 year

Quick Facts
QKFACT VPI   927460105 Vintage Petroleum, Inc.

Market Guide Quick Facts Report

Vintage Petroleum, Inc.	SYMBOL: VPI	EXCHANGE:	NYSE

PRICING DATA (AS OF)	07/14/00	RATIOS & STATISTICS	
Price	21.19	Price/Revenue (TTM)	2.20
52 Week High	25.13	P/E (TTM)	10.06
52 Week Low	9.06	Price/Book (MRQ)	2.81
Beta	1.57	Price/Cash Flow (TTM)	5.66
Avg Daily Vol (10 Day)	0.42 Mil	ROA (TTM)	12.20%
Avg Daily Vol (3 Month)	0.38 Mil	ROE (TTM)	35.84%
		Current Ratio (MRQ)	1.01
DIVIDEND INFORMATION		Total Debt/Equity (MRQ)	1.10
Indicated Annual ($)	0.12		
Yield	0.57%	NOTE: TTM = trailing twelve months	
		MRQ = most recent quarter	

SHARE RELATED INFORMATION		SHORT INTEREST INFORMATION	
Market Cap. ($)	1,324.038 Mil	Current Month	2.231 Mil
Shares Out.	62.490 Mil	Previous Month	1.625 Mil
Float	44.400 Mil	Short Interest Ratio	5.6 Day

INSTITUTIONAL & INSIDER OWNERSHIP

	PURCHASES	SALES	NET PURCH	%OWNED
Institutions (3 Months)	9.134 Mil	6.941 Mil	2.193 Mil	63.5%
Insiders (6 Months)	0.000 Mil	0.143 Mil	-0.143 Mil	28.9%

BUSINESS SUMMARY

Vintage Petroleum, Inc. is an independent oil and
gas company focused on the acquisition of oil and gas
properties which contain the potential for increased value
through exploitation and exploration. For the 3 months
ended 3/31/00, total revenues rose from $66M to $167.3M.
Net income totalled $42.7M vs. a loss of $18.1M. Results
reflect increased average oil prices and higher oil
production. Earnings reflect improved gross margins.

REVENUES (Thousands of U.S. Dollars)

QUARTERS	1997	1998	1999	2000
MAR	99,234	89,994	66,004	167,322
JUN	99,843	84,932	92,561	
SEP	104,387	79,285	136,429	
DEC	113,126	74,724	201,741	
TOTAL	416,590	328,935	496,735	

EARNINGS PER SHARE

	1997	1998	1999	2000
MAR	0.350	-0.030	-0.340	0.670
JUN	0.210	-0.180	0.090	
SEP	0.260	-0.190	0.430	
DEC	0.240	-1.270	0.920	
TOTAL	1.060	-1.670	1.100	

10/97, 2-for-1 stock split.FY'96-'97 fncls. & FY'97-'98
Q's restated for accounting change.   FY'97, '98 Q's are
reclass. PO 6/99, 9M shs @ $9.50 by Salomon Smith Barney.

GROWTH RATES	1 YEAR	3 YEAR	5 YEAR
Revenue	51.01%	16.75%	21.76%
EPS	NM%	21.95%	30.33%
Dividend	-70.59%	-23.11%	-6.51%

(Load Date: 7/17/00)
Database: Quick Facts
Keyword(s): (VPI)

End of Report

CHART B-3

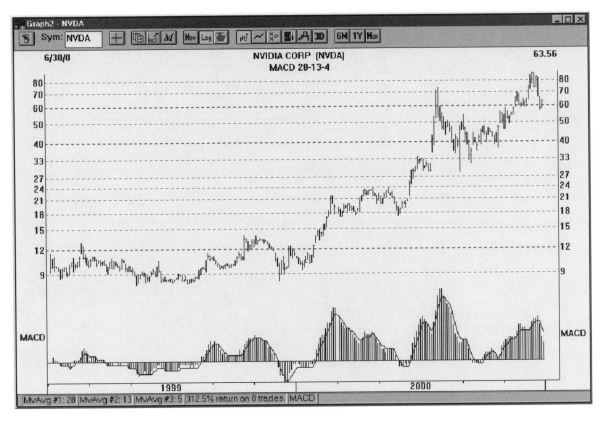

Courtesy of Telescan, Inc.

Nvidia Corporation current 2 year

Quick Facts
QKFACT NVDA   67066G104 NVIDIA Corporation

Market Guide Quick Facts Report

NVIDIA Corporation	SYMBOL: NVDA	EXCHANGE:	NASD

PRICING DATA (AS OF)	07/14/00	RATIOS & STATISTICS	
Price	73.81	Price/Revenue (TTM)	12.07
52 Week High	88.00	P/E (TTM)	110.17
52 Week Low	8.38	Price/Book (MRQ)	29.28
Beta	NA	Price/Cash Flow (TTM)	89.15
Avg Daily Vol (10 Day)	2.25 Mil	ROA (TTM)	23.45%
Avg Daily Vol (3 Month)	1.17 Mil	ROE (TTM)	46.02%
		Current Ratio (MRQ)	4.90
DIVIDEND INFORMATION		Total Debt/Equity (MRQ)	0.01
Indicated Annual ($)	0.00		
Yield	0.00%	NOTE: TTM = trailing twelve months	
		MRQ = most recent quarter	

SHARE RELATED INFORMATION		SHORT INTEREST INFORMATION	
Market Cap. ($)	4,756.805 Mil	Current Month	3.442 Mil
Shares Out.	64.444 Mil	Previous Month	1.680 Mil
Float	46.400 Mil	Short Interest Ratio	1.7 Day

INSTITUTIONAL & INSIDER OWNERSHIP

	PURCHASES	SALES	NET PURCH	%OWNED
Institutions (3 Months)	9.994 Mil	9.578 Mil	0.416 Mil	34.8%
Insiders (6 Months)	0.000 Mil	0.425 Mil	-0.425 Mil	28.0%

BUSINESS SUMMARY
NVIDIA Corporation designs, develops and markets 3D
graphics processors, graphics processing units and related
software for every type of desktop personal computer,
ranging from professional workstations to low-cost PCs.
For the 13 weeks ended 4/30/00, total revenues totaled
$148.5M, up from $71M. Net income totaled $18.3M, up from
$6.3M. Results reflect increased sales of graphics
processors and higher margins due to increased volumes.

REVENUES (Thousands of U.S. Dollars)

QUARTERS	1998	1999	2000	2001
APR	0	28,263	71,018	148,483
JUL	0	12,134	78,017	
OCT	0	52,303	97,015	
JAN	13,331	65,537	128,455	
TOTAL	13,331	158,237	374,505	

EARNINGS PER SHARE

	1998	1999	2000	2001
APR	0.000	-0.035	0.090	0.235
JUL	0.000	-0.340	0.095	
OCT	0.000	0.130	0.145	
JAN	0.025	0.135	0.195	
TOTAL	0.025	-0.110	0.525	

FY'93 = 39 weeks due to 4/5/93 inception of operations.
FY'98 = 4 weeks due to FY end change from DEC to JAN.

GROWTH RATES	1 YEAR	3 YEAR	5 YEAR
Revenue	136.67%	134.42%	216.35%
EPS	604.00%	NM%	NM%
Dividend	NM%	NM%	NM%

(Load Date: 7/17/00)
Database: Quick Facts
Keyword(s): (NVDA)

End of Report

CHART B-4

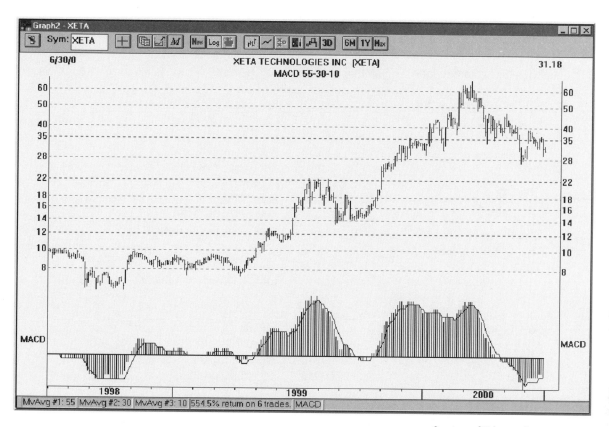

Xeta Technologies, Inc. current 2 year

Quick Facts
QKFACT XETA   983909102 XETA Technologies, Inc.

Market Guide Quick Facts Report

XETA Technologies, Inc.	SYMBOL: XETA	EXCHANGE:	NASD

PRICING DATA (AS OF)	07/14/00	RATIOS & STATISTICS	
Price	30.25	Price/Revenue (TTM)	2.10
52 Week High	67.88	P/E (TTM)	26.03
52 Week Low	13.50	Price/Book (MRQ)	5.79
Beta	0.10	Price/Cash Flow (TTM)	17.84
Avg Daily Vol (10 Day)	0.05 Mil	ROA (TTM)	13.64%
Avg Daily Vol (3 Month)	0.04 Mil	ROE (TTM)	34.29%
		Current Ratio (MRQ)	1.57
DIVIDEND INFORMATION		Total Debt/Equity (MRQ)	1.34
Indicated Annual ($)	0.00		
Yield	0.00%		

NOTE: TTM = trailing twelve months
MRQ = most recent quarter

SHARE RELATED INFORMATION		SHORT INTEREST INFORMATION	
Market Cap. ($)	127.020 Mil	Current Month	0.105 Mil
Shares Out.	4.199 Mil	Previous Month	0.096 Mil
Float	2.600 Mil	Short Interest Ratio	2.3 Day

INSTITUTIONAL & INSIDER OWNERSHIP

	PURCHASES	SALES	NET PURCH	%OWNED
Institutions (3 Months)	0.225 Mil	0.108 Mil	0.117 Mil	10.7%
Insiders (6 Months)	0.003 Mil	0.082 Mil	-0.079 Mil	38.1%

BUSINESS SUMMARY
XETA is a voice and data integrator with offices
and service centers located throughout the U.S. XETA
engages in the sale and servicing of call accounting
systems to the lodging industry. For the 6 months ended
4/30/00, revenues totalled $48M, up from $16.3M. Net income
rose 66% to $3.2M. Results reflect growth in small-of-large
segment and enterprise market, partially offset by higher
SG&A and lower gross margin due to product mix changes.

REVENUES (Thousands of U.S. Dollars)

QUARTERS	1997	1998	1999	2000
JAN	2,901	5,051	7,047	20,550
APR	5,195	6,566	9,241	27,473
JUL	5,299	7,182	9,789	
OCT	5,365	6,648	11,186	
TOTAL	18,760	25,447	37,263	

EARNINGS PER SHARE

	1997	1998	1999	2000
JAN	0.070	0.150	0.170	0.310
APR	0.120	0.170	0.250	0.350
JUL	0.125	0.170	0.240	
OCT	0.135	0.170	0.270	
TOTAL	0.450	0.660	0.930	

2/00, Name changed from XETA Corporation.FY'92 annual weighted average shares outstanding are estimated. FY'98 Q's are reclassified.

GROWTH RATES	1 YEAR	3 YEAR	5 YEAR
Revenue	46.43%	40.48%	38.24%
EPS	42.03%	39.79%	29.83%
Dividend	NM%	NM%	NM%

(Load Date: 7/17/00)
Database: Quick Facts
Keyword(s): (XETA)

End of Report

CHART B-5

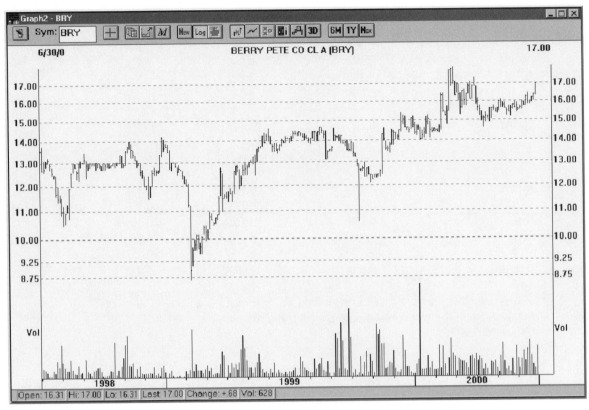

Courtesy of Telescan, Inc.

Berry Petroleum Company current 2 year

Quick Facts
QKFACT BRY   085789105 Berry Petroleum Company   UPDATED

Market Guide Quick Facts Report

Berry Petroleum CompanySYMBOL: BRY   EXCHANGE: NYSE

PRICING DATA (AS OF)	07/14/00	RATIOS & STATISTICS	
Price	18.31	Price/Revenue (TTM)	4.82
52 Week High	18.38	P/E (TTM)	15.38
52 Week Low	12.13	Price/Book (MRQ)	3.28
Beta	0.14	Price/Cash Flow (TTM)	10.35
Avg Daily Vol (10 Day)	0.04 Mil	ROA (TTM)	12.58%
Avg Daily Vol (3 Month)	0.03 Mil	ROE (TTM)	23.46%
		Current Ratio (MRQ)	1.28
DIVIDEND INFORMATION		Total Debt/Equity (MRQ)	0.36
Indicated Annual ($)	0.40		
Yield	2.18%	NOTE: TTM = trailing twelve months	
		MRQ = most recent quarter	

SHARE RELATED INFORMATION		SHORT INTEREST INFORMATION	
Market Cap. ($)	403.417 Mil	Current Month	0.018 Mil
Shares Out.	22.029 Mil	Previous Month	0.009 Mil
Float	11.600 Mil	Short Interest Ratio	0.7 Day

INSTITUTIONAL & INSIDER OWNERSHIP

	PURCHASES	SALES	NET PURCH	%OWNED
Institutions (3 Months)	0.992 Mil	0.630 Mil	0.362 Mil	38.8%
Insiders (6 Months)	0.000 Mil	0.042 Mil	-0.042 Mil	47.3%

BUSINESS SUMMARY
Berry Petroleum Company is engaged in the
acquisition, exploration, exploitation, development,
production, and marketing of crude oil and natural gas. For
the 3 months ended 03/31/00, revenues totalled $26.1M up
from $9.7M. Net income totalled $8.9M, up from $544K.
Revenues reflect higher oil prices and higher production.
Net income also reflects reduced operating expenses as a
percentage of revenues.

REVENUES (Thousands of U.S. Dollars)

QUARTERS	1997	1998	1999	2000
MAR	17,581	11,576	9,657	26,137
JUN	16,240	9,455	14,561	
SEP	17,658	10,120	19,360	
DEC	17,516	8,748	23,897	
TOTAL	68,995	39,899	67,475	

EARNINGS PER SHARE

MAR	0.220	0.090	0.020	0.400
JUN	0.210	0.070	0.150	
SEP	0.230	0.060	0.280	
DEC	0.210	-0.050	0.370	
TOTAL	0.870	0.170	0.820	

FY'92, FY'93, FY'94 financials are reclassified.   FY'96
financials are reclassified.FY'97 Q's are reclass.

GROWTH RATES	1 YEAR	3 YEAR	5 YEAR
Revenue	69.11%	5.62%	10.30%
EPS	364.21%	0.75%	10.10%
Dividend	0.00%	0.00%	0.00%

(Load Date: 7/17/00)
Database: Quick Facts
Keyword(s): (BRY)

End of Report

CHART B-6

Courtesy of Telescan, Inc.

Imperial Oil Limited current 2 year

Quick Facts
QKFACT IMO   453038408 Imperial Oil Limited

Market Guide Quick Facts Report

Imperial Oil Limited	SYMBOL: IMO	EXCHANGE:	AMEX

PRICING DATA (AS OF)	07/14/00	RATIOS & STATISTICS	
Price	24.63	Price/Revenue (TTM)	1.26
52 Week High	26.38	P/E (TTM)	19.78
52 Week Low	17.94	Price/Book (MRQ)	3.47
Beta	0.40	Price/Cash Flow (TTM)	10.75
Avg Daily Vol (10 Day)	0.08 Mil	ROA (TTM)	7.90%
Avg Daily Vol (3 Month)	0.08 Mil	ROE (TTM)	18.41%
		Current Ratio (MRQ)	1.21
DIVIDEND INFORMATION		Total Debt/Equity (MRQ)	0.28
Indicated Annual ($)	0.00		
Yield	0.00%	NOTE: TTM = trailing twelve months	
		MRQ = most recent quarter	

SHARE RELATED INFORMATION		SHORT INTEREST INFORMATION	
Market Cap. ($)	10,520.785 Mil	Current Month	0.208 Mil
Shares Out.	427.240 Mil	Previous Month	0.197 Mil
Float	123.900 Mil	Short Interest Ratio	2.4 Day

INSTITUTIONAL & INSIDER OWNERSHIP

	PURCHASES	SALES	NET PURCH	%OWNED
Institutions (3 Months)	9.426 Mil	6.904 Mil	2.522 Mil	9.4%
Insiders (6 Months)	0.000 Mil	0.000 Mil	0.000 Mil	71.0%

BUSINESS SUMMARY
Imperial Oil Limited produces crude oil and natural
gas, refines and markets petroleum products under the name
Esso, and is a supplier of petrochemicals and fertilizers.
For the 3 months ended 3/31/00, total revenues rose 67% to
C$4.07B. Net income totalled C$269M, up from C$37M.
Revenues reflect increased natural gas production from the
Sable Offshore Energy Project. Earnings also benefitted
from the unchanged corporate and other expenses.

ADR INFORMATION
Shares Per ADR   1.000
Most Recent Currency Rate   1.484

REVENUES (Millions of Canadian Dollars)

QUARTERS	1997	1998	1999	2000
MAR	2,696	2,238	2,419	4,066
JUN	2,643	2,319	2,419	
SEP	2,729	2,344	2,793	
DEC	3,054	2,244	3,164	
TOTAL	11,122	9,145	10,795	

EARNINGS PER SHARE

MAR	0.400	0.250	0.090	0.630
JUN	0.390	0.250	0.220	
SEP	0.440	0.450	0.480	
DEC	0.600	0.310	0.510	
TOTAL	1.830	1.260	1.300	

FY'91 - FY'96 financials, & FY'94 and FY'96 - '97 summ. Q's
are reclassified.FY'97 Q's are reclassified.   FY'88
- '90 financials are restated for acctg. change.

GROWTH RATES	1 YEAR	3 YEAR	5 YEAR
Revenue	13.16%	-0.49%	2.84%
EPS	6.79%	-4.34%	26.71%
Dividend	1.35%	3.15%	-14.06%

(Load Date: 7/17/00)
Database: Quick Facts
Keyword(s): (IMO)

End of Report

CHART B-7

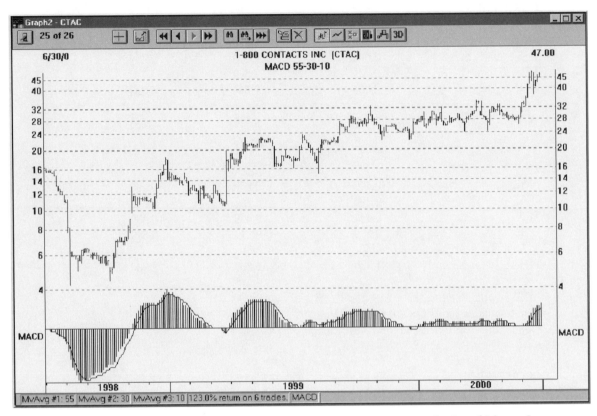

Courtesy of Telescan, Inc.

1-800 Contacts, Inc. current 2 year

Quick Facts
QKFACT CTAC   681977104 1-800 CONTACTS, INC.

Market Guide Quick Facts Report

1-800 CONTACTS, INC.	SYMBOL: CTAC	EXCHANGE:	NASD

PRICING DATA (AS OF)	07/14/00	RATIOS & STATISTICS	
Price	50.75	Price/Revenue (TTM)	2.99
52 Week High	51.00	P/E (TTM)	42.15
52 Week Low	15.25	Price/Book (MRQ)	18.75
Beta	2.75	Price/Cash Flow (TTM)	36.83
Avg Daily Vol (10 Day)	0.07 Mil	ROA (TTM)	30.79%
Avg Daily Vol (3 Month)	0.07 Mil	ROE (TTM)	48.52%
		Current Ratio (MRQ)	2.20
DIVIDEND INFORMATION		Total Debt/Equity (MRQ)	0.00
Indicated Annual ($)	0.00		
Yield	0.00%	NOTE: TTM = trailing twelve months	
		MRQ = most recent quarter	

SHARE RELATED INFORMATION		SHORT INTEREST INFORMATION	
Market Cap. ($)	306.073 Mil	Current Month	0.772 Mil
Shares Out.	6.031 Mil	Previous Month	0.802 Mil
Float	2.200 Mil	Short Interest Ratio	8.8 Day

INSTITUTIONAL & INSIDER OWNERSHIP

	PURCHASES	SALES	NET PURCH	%OWNED
Institutions (3 Months)	0.319 Mil	0.294 Mil	0.025 Mil	23.1%
Insiders (6 Months)	0.000 Mil	0.017 Mil	-0.017 Mil	63.5%

BUSINESS SUMMARY
1-800 CONTACTS is a direct marketer of replacement
contact lenses. Through its toll-free telephone number, it
sells substantially all of the most popular brands of
contact lenses. For the 13 weeks ended 4/1/2000, revenues
rose 41% to $31.4M. Net income totalled $1.8M, up from
$297K. Revenues benefitted from repeat sales of the
customer base. Earnings reflect competitive pricing and
enhanced inventory management techniques.

REVENUES (Thousands of U.S. Dollars)

QUARTERS	1997	1998	1999	2000
MAR	2,846	10,429	22,304	31,419
JUN	4,870	12,800	23,960	
SEP	6,428	18,419	26,890	
DEC	6,971	18,228	25,371	
TOTAL	21,115	59,876	98,525	

EARNINGS PER SHARE

MAR	0.030	0.080	0.050	0.290
JUN	0.040	-0.140	0.230	
SEP	0.040	-0.380	0.160	
DEC	0.030	-0.780	0.520	
TOTAL	0.140	-1.220	0.960	

Financials and weighted average share amounts prior to IPO
are pro forma.FY'95 = 11 months (from date of inception
2/1/95).   FY'98 Q's are restated.

GROWTH RATES	1 YEAR	3 YEAR	5 YEAR
Revenue	64.55%	200.58%	259.78%
EPS	NM%	177.44%	NM%
Dividend	NM%	NM%	NM%

(Load Date: 7/17/00)
Database: Quick Facts
Keyword(s): (CTAC)

End of Report

CHART B-8

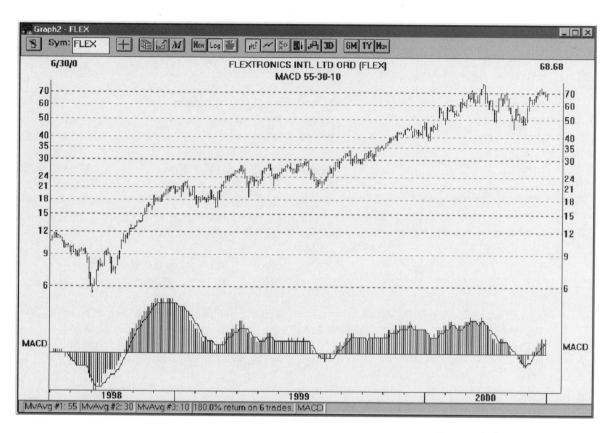

Courtesy of Telescan, Inc.

Flextronics International, LTD. current 2 year

Quick Facts
QKFACT FLEX   Y2573F102 Flextronics International

Market Guide Quick Facts Report

Flextronics International	SYMBOL: FLEX	EXCHANGE:	NASD

PRICING DATA (AS OF)	07/14/00	RATIOS & STATISTICS	
Price	83.75	Price/Revenue (TTM)	2.31
52 Week High	84.81	P/E (TTM)	83.17
52 Week Low	21.25	Price/Book (MRQ)	6.61
Beta	2.60	Price/Cash Flow (TTM)	77.98
Avg Daily Vol (10 Day)	2.50 Mil	ROA (TTM)	6.41%
Avg Daily Vol (3 Month)	3.35 Mil	ROE (TTM)	14.39%
		Current Ratio (MRQ)	1.83
DIVIDEND INFORMATION		Total Debt/Equity (MRQ)	0.31
Indicated Annual ($)	NM		
Yield	NA%	NOTE: TTM = trailing twelve months	
		MRQ = most recent quarter	

SHARE RELATED INFORMATION		SHORT INTEREST INFORMATION	
Market Cap. ($)	16,226.395 Mil	Current Month	2.842 Mil
Shares Out.	193.748 Mil	Previous Month	2.020 Mil
Float	127.900 Mil	Short Interest Ratio	0.8 Day

INSTITUTIONAL & INSIDER OWNERSHIP

	PURCHASES	SALES	NET PURCH	%OWNED
Institutions (3 Months)	30.291 Mil	9.818 Mil	20.472 Mil	59.8%
Insiders (6 Months)	0.000 Mil	0.703 Mil	-0.703 Mil	34.0%

BUSINESS SUMMARY

Flextronics International provides electronics
manufacturing services to OEMs in the networking, computer,
medical, consumer and telecommunications industries. For
the FY ended 3/31/00, net sales rose 93% to $4.31B. Net
income rose 99% to $120.9M. Revenues reflect the Company's
ability to expand sales to new customers worldwide and
increased sales at existing customers. Earnings also
reflect a reduction in unusual charges.

REVENUES (Thousands of U.S. Dollars)

QUARTERS	1997	1998	1999	2000
JUN	149,782	235,545	427,501	685,641
SEP	156,757	251,468	515,394	941,760
DEC	161,248	295,000	631,932	1,251,681
MAR	172,220	331,058	658,381	1,428,111
TOTAL	640,007	1,113,071	2,233,208	4,307,193

EARNINGS PER SHARE

JUN	0.075	0.095	0.140	0.170
SEP	0.085	0.090	0.170	0.250
DEC	-0.003	0.075	0.180	0.310
MAR	0.013	0.010	0.140	0.270
TOTAL	0.170	0.270	0.630	1.000

FY'98-'99 and FY'99-'00 Q's are restated for poolings with PCB Assembly and Kyrel EMS.4/3/00, Company acquired The Dii Group for 62,768,139 shares (pooling of interests).

GROWTH RATES	1 YEAR	3 YEAR	5 YEAR
Revenue	92.87%	88.80%	71.28%
EPS	63.00%	82.55%	52.97%
Dividend	NM%	NM%	NM%

(Load Date: 7/17/00)
Database: Quick Facts
Keyword(s): (FLEX)

End of Report

CHART B-9

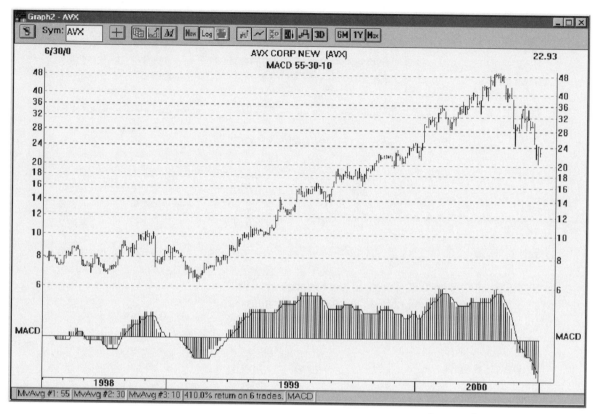

Courtesy of Telescan, Inc.

AVX Corporation current 2 year

Quick Facts
QKFACT AVX   002444107 AVX Corporation   UPDATED

Market Guide Quick Facts Report

AVX Corporation	SYMBOL: AVX	EXCHANGE:	NYSE

PRICING DATA (AS OF)	07/14/00	RATIOS & STATISTICS	
Price	28.56	Price/Revenue (TTM)	2.66*
52 Week High	50.00	P/E (TTM)	19.40*
52 Week Low	13.88	Price/Book (MRQ)	5.08
Beta	0.72	Price/Cash Flow (TTM)	19.51
Avg Daily Vol (10 Day)	1.91 Mil	ROA (TTM)	21.71%*
Avg Daily Vol (3 Month)	0.93 Mil	ROE (TTM)	28.76%*
		Current Ratio (MRQ)	3.00
DIVIDEND INFORMATION		Total Debt/Equity (MRQ)	0.03
Indicated Annual ($)	0.14		
Yield	0.49%	NOTE: TTM = trailing twelve months	
		MRQ = most recent quarter	

SHARE RELATED INFORMATION		SHORT INTEREST INFORMATION	
Market Cap. ($)	4,947.140 Mil	Current Month	0.659 Mil
Shares Out.	173.201 Mil	Previous Month	0.372 Mil
Float	50.200 Mil	Short Interest Ratio	0.9 Day

INSTITUTIONAL & INSIDER OWNERSHIP

	PURCHASES	SALES	NET PURCH	%OWNED
Institutions (3 Months)	16.426 Mil	6.101 Mil	10.325 Mil	31.3%
Insiders (6 Months)	0.000 Mil	5.507 Mil	-5.507 Mil	71.0%

BUSINESS SUMMARY
AVX Corp. manufactures and supplies a broad line of
passive electronic components and related products. The
Co. also manufactures and sells electronic connectors. For
the FY ended 3/31/00, net sales rose 31% to $1.63B. Net
income totalled $156.9M, up from $41.5M. Revenues reflect
increased demand in telecommunications and IT hardware
industries. Earnings also benefitted from favorable pricing
environment and improvement in manufacturing process.

PRELIMINARY: For the 3 months ended 06/30/2000, revenues
were 602,448; after tax earnings were 120,436. (expressed in Thousands)

REVENUES (Thousands of U.S. Dollars)

QUARTERS	1998	1999	2000	2001
JUN	313,807	292,000	343,150	602,448*
SEP	329,224	324,144	371,573	
DEC	319,651	310,718	416,412	
MAR	304,971	318,611	499,138	
TOTAL	1,267,653	1,245,473	1,630,273	

EARNINGS PER SHARE

	1998	1999	2000	2001
JUN	0.200	0.100	0.100	0.680*
SEP	0.205	0.060	0.150	
DEC	0.190	0.030	0.240	
MAR	0.168	0.040	0.400	
TOTAL	0.763	0.230	0.890	

FY'95 quarterly dividend number = 12 months. Number of common stock holders for 1999 represent beneficial holders.

GROWTH RATES	1 YEAR	3 YEAR	5 YEAR
Revenue	30.90%	13.12%	10.52%
EPS	276.89%	9.19%	15.52%
Dividend	0.00%	4.94%	-3.46%

(Load Date: 7/17/00)
Database: Quick Facts
Keyword(s): (AVX)

End of Report

CHART B-10

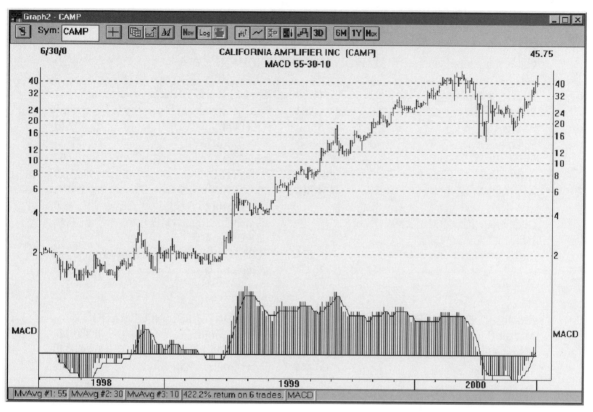

California Amplifier, Inc. current 2 year

Quick Facts
QKFACT CAMP   129900106 California Amplifier   UPDATED

Market Guide Quick Facts Report

California Amplifier	SYMBOL: CAMP	EXCHANGE:	NASD

PRICING DATA (AS OF)	07/14/00	RATIOS & STATISTICS	
Price	42.94	Price/Revenue (TTM)	5.50
52 Week High	63.00	P/E (TTM)	NM
52 Week Low	7.50	Price/Book (MRQ)	17.20
Beta	1.53	Price/Cash Flow (TTM)	159.03
Avg Daily Vol (10 Day)	1.08 Mil	ROA (TTM)	0.84%
Avg Daily Vol (3 Month)	0.51 Mil	ROE (TTM)	1.45%
		Current Ratio (MRQ)	2.30
DIVIDEND INFORMATION		Total Debt/Equity (MRQ)	0.16
Indicated Annual ($)	0.00		
Yield	0.00%	NOTE: TTM = trailing twelve months	
		MRQ = most recent quarter	

SHARE RELATED INFORMATION		SHORT INTEREST INFORMATION	
Market Cap. ($)	568.714 Mil	Current Month	0.280 Mil
Shares Out.	13.245 Mil	Previous Month	0.241 Mil
Float	11.700 Mil	Short Interest Ratio	0.9 Day

INSTITUTIONAL & INSIDER OWNERSHIP

	PURCHASES	SALES	NET PURCH	%OWNED
Institutions (3 Months)	2.401 Mil	1.186 Mil	1.215 Mil	44.4%
Insiders (6 Months)	0.005 Mil	0.000 Mil	0.005 Mil	11.7%

BUSINESS SUMMARY
California Amplifier designs, manufactures, and
markets microwave products used in the reception of video
transmitted from satellites or wireless terrestrial sites
and antennas used in global positioning systems. For the
3 months ended 05/27/00, revenues totaled $32.3M, up from
$13.1M. Net income totalled $2.1M, up from $358K. Results
reflect increased Satellite product sales and improved
gross profit margin.

REVENUES (Thousands of U.S. Dollars)

QUARTERS	1998	1999	2000	2001
MAY	12,013	9,060	13,093	32,284
AUG	13,091	8,322	18,575	
NOV	13,382	9,681	26,251	
FEB	8,447	10,077	27,709	
TOTAL	46,933	37,140	85,628	

EARNINGS PER SHARE

MAY	0.010	-0.040	0.030	0.150
AUG	0.020	-0.070	0.070	
NOV	-0.080	-0.020	0.120	
FEB	-0.180	0.010	-0.340	
TOTAL	-0.230	-0.120	-0.120	

During the 2nd Q. of FY'91, the Company privately placed 378K shares @ $1.13/share.2/99 & 11/98 quarterly balance sheet and cash flow were reclassified.

GROWTH RATES	1 YEAR	3 YEAR	5 YEAR
Revenue	130.56%	20.21%	13.40%
EPS	NM%	NM%	NM%
Dividend	NM%	NM%	NM%

(Load Date: 7/17/00)
Database: Quick Facts
Keyword(s): (CAMP)

End of Report

Search 2 (MAGNET® Complex) Results— TOP THIRTY-TWO STOCKS, AS LISTED BY TELESCAN

```
*******************************

      Prosearch 5.0* Top Stock Report

                06/14/00

*******************************
```

1>   CXP   - CENTEX CONSTR PRODS INC   .BBC
Price= 28.8   Capzn= 54.9   %InsH= 33.6   Currt= 2.6
%D/Eq= 0.1   RelPE= 4.0 $/Sls= 1.3   3LDv = -19.2
C/IGr= 1.6   C/SGr= 3.0 $Rank= 775.6   EPSRk= 98.0
AcDst= 66.0   ERG= 85.8   cERG3= 61.2   6-Wk = 1796.8
1-Yr = 5750.0 1YrSa= 34.9   1YrEg= 51.7

2>   MAIR   - MESABA HLDGS INC   .ATR
Price= 10.8   Capzn= 21.2   %InsH= 39.1   Currt= 2.9
%D/Eq= 3.3   RelPE= 17.4 $/Sls= 0.5   3LDv = -14.7
C/IGr= 2.6   C/SGr= 4.6 $Rank= 375.6   EPSRk= 83.0
AcDst= 68.0   ERG= 79.3   cERG3= 63.7   6-Wk = 671.8
1-Yr = 2150.0 1YrSa= 25.5   1YrEg= 44.6

3>   TKS   - TOMKINS PLC ADR SPONSORED   .CDI
Price= 11.6   Capzn= 280.8   %InsH= 8.0   Currt= 1.6
%D/Eq= 0.0   RelPE= 0.0 $/Sls= 0.4   3LDv = -10.4
C/IGr= 2.0   C/SGr= 1.6 $Rank= 395.1   EPSRk= 87.0
AcDst= 66.0   ERG= 58.6   cERG3= 56.0   6-Wk = 726.8
1-Yr = 2326.0 1YrSa= 27.4   1YrEg= 23.8

4>   DG   - DOLLAR GEN CORP   .RDI
Price= 16.3   Capzn= 680.7   %InsH= 53.3   Currt= 2.1
%D/Eq= 20.4 RelPE= 8.2 $/Sls= 1.4   3LDv = -6.7
C/IGr= 2.1   C/SGr= 2.2 $Rank= 499.2   EPSRk= 92.0
AcDst= 81.0   ERG= 68.6   cERG3= 40.2   6-Wk = 1019.3
1-Yr = 3262.0 1YrSa= 30.0   1YrEg= 19.6

5>   TRR   - TRC COS INC   .POL
Price= 10.3   Capzn= 7.0   %InsH= 27.0   Currt= 1.9
%D/Eq= 19.8 RelPE= 6.1 $/Sls= 1.0   3LDv = 12.7
C/IGr= N/A   C/SGr= N/A $Rank= 365.9   EPSRk= 99.0
AcDst= 56.0   ERG= 76.1   cERG3= 78.7   6-Wk = 644.3
1-Yr = 2062.0 1YrSa= 36.7   1YrEg= 90.0

6>   MSS   - MEASUREMENT SPECIALTIES INC   .SPE
Price= 33.5   Capzn= 12.3   %InsH= 27.5   Currt= 1.9
%D/Eq= 26.5 RelPE= 8.0 $/Sls= 2.3   3LDv = 30.4
C/IGr= N/A   C/SGr= N/A $Rank= 881.2   EPSRk= 93.0
AcDst= 77.0 ERG= 94.0   cERG3= 93.5   6-Wk = 2093.7
1-Yr = 6700.0 1YrSa= 37.0   1YrEg= 178.2

7>   TSM   - TAIWAN SEMICONDUCTOR MFG CO ADR SP .ESE
Price= 38.6   Capzn= 5844.0   %InsH= 4.8   Currt= 2.7
%D/Eq= 16.6 RelPE= N/A $/Sls= 24.0   3LDv = N/A
C/IGr= 1.4   C/SGr= 1.3 $Rank= 993.7   EPSRk= 98.0
AcDst= 86.0 ERG= 96.0   cERG3= 95.2   6-Wk = 2410.0
1-Yr = 7712.0 1YrSa= 82.6   1YrEg= 161.9

8>   QLGC   - QLOGIC CORP   .ESE
Price= 53.9   Capzn= 412.1   %InsH= 73.2   Currt= 6.3
%D/Eq= 0.0 RelPE= 31.8 $/Sls= 21.6   3LDv = -46.0
C/IGr= 0.7   C/SGr= 0.7 $Rank= 1335.4 EPSRk= 99.0
AcDst= 88.0 ERG= 97.5   cERG3= 97.0   6-Wk = 3371.2
1-Yr = 10788.0 1YrSa= 66.2   1YrEg= 100.0

9>   TTIL   - TTI TEAM TELECOM INTL LTD ORD   .DSO
Price= 30.8   Capzn= 23.4   %InsH= 36.7   Currt= 4.7
%D/Eq= 0.0 RelPE= N/A $/Sls= 9.3   3LDv = 33.8
C/IGr= 2.0   C/SGr= 1.8 $Rank= 820.1   EPSRk= 95.0
AcDst= 78.0 ERG= 73.1   cERG3= 56.2   6-Wk = 1921.8
1-Yr = 6150.0 1YrSa= 42.6   1YrEg= 55.5

10>   AVX   - AVX CORP NEW   .ECC
Price= 33.0   Capzn= 575.0   %InsH= 15.5   Currt= 3.0
%D/Eq= 3.7 RelPE= 49.0 $/Sls= 3.6   3LDv = 46.6
C/IGr= 0.8   C/SGr= 0.8 $Rank= 870.1   EPSRk= 94.0
AcDst= 83.0 ERG= 81.8   cERG3= 79.2   6-Wk = 2062.5
1-Yr = 6600.0 1YrSa= 32.6   1YrEg= 256.0

11>   CBXC   - CYBEX COMPUTER PRODS CORP   .DCS
Price= 39.3   Capzn= 76.1   %InsH= 60.3   Currt= 4.1
%D/Eq= 0.0 RelPE= 62.3 $/Sls= 6.7   3LDv = 8.9
C/IGr= 1.1   C/SGr= 1.2 $Rank= 1010.4 EPSRk= 93.0
AcDst= 75.0 ERG= 74.0   cERG3= 68.2   6-Wk = 2456.8
1-Yr = 7862.0 1YrSa= 48.7   1YrEg= 43.7

12>   FLEX   - FLEXTRONICS INTL LTD ORD   .MAN
Price= 65.8   Capzn= 728.2   %InsH= 95.0   Currt= 1.8
%D/Eq= 37.7 RelPE= 85.5 $/Sls= 1.9   3LDv = 11.7
C/IGr= 1.0   C/SGr= 1.0 $Rank= 1599.2 EPSRk= 99.0
AcDst= 88.0 ERG= 79.0   cERG3= 63.7   6-Wk = 4113.1
1-Yr = 13162.0 1YrSa= 82.3   1YrEg= 69.0

13>   TOPP   - TOPPS INC   .LSC
      Price= 10.1   Capzn= 46.4   %InsH= 37.2   Currt= 1.8
      %D/Eq= 0.0   RelPE= 3.0 $/Sls= 1.3   3LDv = -3.9
      C/IGr= N/A   C/SGr= N/A $Rank= 361.8   EPSRk= 99.0
      AcDst= 78.0   ERG= 59.8   cERG3= 42.2   6-Wk = 633.1
      1-Yr = 2026.0 1YrSa= 62.4   1YrEg= 278.7

14>   ATYT   - ATI TECHNOLOGIES INC   .DSO
      Price= 10.8   Capzn= 222.0   %InsH= 15.2   Currt= 2.4
      %D/Eq= 0.0   RelPE= N/A $/Sls= 1.7   3LDv = N/A
      C/IGr= 1.5   C/SGr= 1.6 $Rank= 377.0   EPSRk= 98.0
      AcDst= 66.0   ERG= 67.3   cERG3= 46.0   6-Wk = 675.6
      1-Yr = 2162.0 1YrSa= 51.0   1YrEg= 77.7

15>   NOK   - NOKIA CORP ADR SPONSORED   .TES
      Price= 58.8   Capzn= 28496.6 %InsH= 28.1   Currt= 1.7
      %D/Eq= 14.4   RelPE= 98.9 $/Sls= 13.0   3LDv = 5.4
      C/IGr= 0.8   C/SGr= 0.7 $Rank= 1443.7   EPSRk= 99.0
      AcDst= 90.0   ERG= 81.1   cERG3= 88.0   6-Wk = 3675.6
      1-Yr = 11762.0 1YrSa= 48.8   1YrEg= 51.2

16>   SANM   - SANMINA CORP   .ECC
      Price= 75.5   Capzn= 1753.0   %InsH= 94.9   Currt= 4.9
      %D/Eq= 28.2   RelPE= 64.8 $/Sls= 5.7   3LDv = 25.9
      C/IGr= 1.0   C/SGr= 1.0 $Rank= 1814.5   EPSRk= 94.0
      AcDst= 83.0   ERG= 84.3   cERG3= 83.0   6-Wk = 4718.7
      1-Yr = 15100.0 1YrSa= 135.0   1YrEg= 75.7

17>   BBOX   - BLACK BOX CORP   .DSE
      Price= 81.1   Capzn= 158.9   %InsH= 80.7   Currt= 2.4
      %D/Eq= 35.6   RelPE= 98.2 $/Sls= 3.1   3LDv = 35.3
      C/IGr= 6.0   C/SGr= 1.1 $Rank= 1938.1   EPSRk= 92.0
      AcDst= 79.0   ERG= 65.3   cERG3= 69.5   6-Wk = 5066.2
      1-Yr = 16212.0 1YrSa= 46.9   1YrEg= 23.3

18>   MITY   - MITY-LITE INC   .HFU
      Price= 13.9   Capzn= 6.6   %InsH= 7.4   Currt= 4.2
      %D/Eq= 2.0   RelPE= 18.1 $/Sls= 1.5   3LDv = -21.4
      C/IGr= N/A   C/SGr= N/A $Rank= 446.4   EPSRk= 92.0
      AcDst= 61.0   ERG= 67.0   cERG3= 43.7   6-Wk = 871.2
      1-Yr = 2788.0 1YrSa= 59.3   1YrEg= 17.9

19>   RHI   - ROBERT HALF INTL INC   .SER
      Price= 29.9   Capzn= 537.2   %InsH= 72.6   Currt= 2.7
      %D/Eq= 0.4   RelPE= 37.0 $/Sls= 1.2   3LDv = 73.0
      C/IGr= 0.6   C/SGr= 1.2 $Rank= 802.0   EPSRk= 89.0
      AcDst= 83.0   ERG= 67.0   cERG3= 71.5   6-Wk = 1871.2
      1-Yr = 5988.0 1YrSa= 100.1   1YrEg= 10.9

20> KEM   - KEMET CORP   .ECC
Price= 34.3   Capzn= 302.2   %InsH= 45.6   Currt= 1.7
%D/Eq= 31.3 RelPE= 50.3 $/Sls= 3.8   3LDv = 105.0
C/IGr= 0.6   C/SGr= 0.6 $Rank= 899.2   EPSRk= 91.0
AcDst= 88.0   ERG= 81.0   cERG3= 79.5   6-Wk = 2144.3
1-Yr = 6862.0 1YrSa= 39.3   1YrEg= 844.4

21> GMST   - GEMSTAR INTERNATIONL GRP LTD ORD   .ERT
Price= 52.7   Capzn= 532.5   %InsH= 51.0   Currt= 7.5
%D/Eq= 0.0   RelPE= N/A $/Sls= 54.7   3LDv = -30.9
C/IGr= 0.6   C/SGr= 0.6 $Rank= 1307.6   EPSRk= 83.0
AcDst= 88.0   ERG= 67.5   cERG3= 60.5   6-Wk = 3293.1
1-Yr = 10538.0 1YrSa= 32.9   1YrEg= 26.4

22> LOGIY   - LOGITECH INTL S A ADR SPONSORED   .DCO
Price= 61.4   Capzn= 116.1   %InsH= 4.5   Currt= 1.7
%D/Eq= 6.2   RelPE= N/A $/Sls= 2.0   3LDv = 84.4
C/IGr= N/A   C/SGr= N/A $Rank= 1500.6   EPSRk= 83.0
AcDst= 70.0   ERG= 71.6   cERG3= 60.0   6-Wk = 3836.2
1-Yr = 12276.0 1YrSa= 44.3   1YrEg= 302.9

23> DTPI   - DIAMOND TECHNOLGY PRTNRS INC CL A   .SER
Price= 74.2   Capzn= 150.9   %InsH= 71.6   Currt= 4.3
%D/Eq= 1.3   RelPE= N/A $/Sls= 14.0   3LDv = 24.3
C/IGr= 0.3   C/SGr= 0.6 $Rank= 1785.4   EPSRk= 98.0
AcDst= 76.0   ERG= 73.0   cERG3= 76.0   6-Wk = 4636.8
1-Yr = 14838.0 1YrSa= 48.0   1YrEg= 47.6

24> TFS   - THREE-FIVE SYS INC   .ESE
Price= 74.3   Capzn= 153.4   %InsH= N/A   Currt= 4.3
%D/Eq= 0.0   RelPE= 78.6 $/Sls= 7.8   3LDv = 260.2
C/IGr= 0.7   C/SGr= 0.8 $Rank= 1788.1   EPSRk= 93.0
AcDst= 76.0   ERG= 96.1   cERG3= 98.0   6-Wk = 4644.3
1-Yr = 14862.0 1YrSa= 50.0   1YrEg= 933.3

25> ANEN   - ANAREN MICROWAVE INC   .EDE
Price= 109.9 Capzn= 86.7   %InsH= 79.4   Currt= 18.5
%D/Eq= 0.0   RelPE= 36.9 $/Sls= 11.5   3LDv = 181.7
C/IGr= 0.5   C/SGr= 0.5 $Rank= 2578.4   EPSRk= 96.0
AcDst= 78.0   ERG= 83.8   cERG3= 92.7   6-Wk = 6867.5
1-Yr = 21976.0 1YrSa= 50.0   1YrEg= 47.4

26> INFY   - INFOSYS TECHNOLOGIES LTD ADR SPON   .DSO
Price= 183.5 Capzn= 2590.0   %InsH= 1.2   Currt= 7.6
%D/Eq= 0.0   RelPE= N/A $/Sls= 120.1   3LDv = N/A
C/IGr= 0.2   C/SGr= 0.2 $Rank= 4214.5   EPSRk= 97.0
AcDst= 75.0   ERG= 77.1   cERG3= 61.2   6-Wk = 11468.7
1-Yr = 36700.0 1YrSa= 35.1   1YrEg= 220.0

27> PRVT   - PRIVATE MEDIA GROUP INC   .PPE
     Price= 10.9 Capzn= 28.7   %InsH= 0.5   Currt= 4.5
     %D/Eq= 0.2   RelPE= N/A $/Sls= 7.2   3LDv = -4.1
     C/IGr= N/A   C/SGr= N/A $Rank= 378.4   EPSRk= 91.0
     AcDst= 61.0 ERG= 63.0   cERG3= 69.7   6-Wk = 680.0
     1-Yr = 2176.0 1YrSa= 245.5   1YrEg= -16.2

28> CHKP   - CHECK POINT SOFTWARE TECH LT ORD   .DSO
     Price= 221.9 Capzn= 1707.6   %InsH= 51.6   Currt= 2.8
     %D/Eq= 0.0   RelPE= N/A $/Sls= 85.9   3LDv = 93.9
     C/IGr= 0.7   C/SGr= 0.5 $Rank= 5067.3   EPSRk= 97.0
     AcDst= 86.0 ERG= 77.1   cERG3= 61.2   6-Wk = 13867.5
     1-Yr = 44376.0 1YrSa= 33.7   1YrEg= 27.1

29> ELRNF   - ELRON ELECTR INDS LTD ORD   .ELE
     Price= 36.0 Capzn= 73.1   %InsH= N/A   Currt= 5.5
     %D/Eq= 18.9 RelPE= 26.6 $/Sls= 6.2   3LDv = 10.0
     C/IGr= N/A   C/SGr= N/A $Rank= 936.8   EPSRk= 91.0
     AcDst= 64.0 ERG= 80.5   cERG3= 86.0   6-Wk = 2250.0
     1-Yr = 7200.0 1YrSa= 80.6   1YrEg= N/A

30> AMCC   - APPLIED MICRO CIRCUITS CORP CDT-CO   .ESE
     Price= 88.9 Capzn= 941.4   %InsH= 73.6   Currt= 6.0
     %D/Eq= 5.0   RelPE= N/A $/Sls= 60.6   3LDv = N/A
     C/IGr= N/A   C/SGr= N/A $Rank= 2111.8   EPSRk= 99.0
     AcDst= 90.0 ERG= 98.3   cERG3= 98.2   6-Wk = 5555.0
     1-Yr = 17776.0 1YrSa= 41.2   1YrEg= 156.2

31> FLSH   - M-SYS FLASH DISK PIONEER LTD ORD   .DCS
     Price= 78.8 Capzn= 77.3   %InsH= 42.1   Currt= 3.0
     %D/Eq= 0.0   RelPE= N/A $/Sls= 24.6   3LDv = 189.0
     C/IGr= 1.2   C/SGr= 0.5 $Rank= 1886.8   EPSRk= 81.0
     AcDst= 79.0 ERG= 71.6   cERG3= 70.7   6-Wk = 4921.8
     1-Yr = 15750.0 1YrSa= 81.1   1YrEg= N/A

32> PRSF   - PORTAL SOFTWARE INC   .DSO
     Price= 51.7 Capzn= 775.1   %InsH= 44.6   Currt= 4.3
     %D/Eq= 1.1   RelPE= N/A $/Sls= 54.7   3LDv = N/A
     C/IGr= N/A   C/SGr= 0.1 $Rank= 1285.4   EPSRk= 90.0
     AcDst= 79.0 ERG= 73.5   cERG3= 59.2   6-Wk = 3230.6
     1-Yr = 10338.0 1YrSa= 28.8   1YrEg= N/A

The above report is based on mathematical calculations and, as such, no investment decision should be based solely on its conclusions.

Telescan Charts and Market Guide "Quick facts" for Search 2 "Top Ten" Stocks

CHART B-11

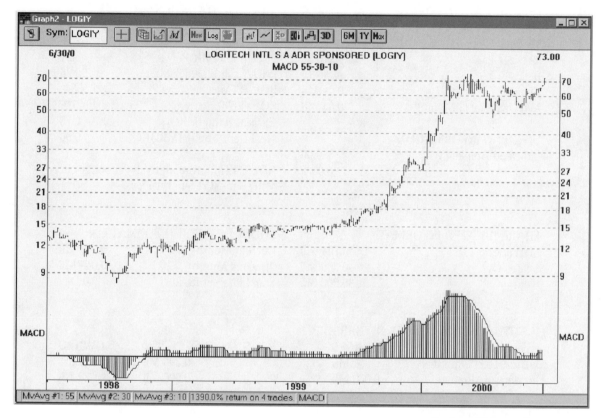

Courtesy of Telescan, Inc.

Logitech International SA current 2 year

Quick Facts
QKFACT LOGIY   541419107 Logitech International SA

Market Guide Quick Facts Report

Logitech International SA   SYMBOL: LOGIY   EXCHANGE: NASD

PRICING DATA (AS OF)	07/14/00	RATIOS & STATISTICS	
Price	35.88	Price/Revenue (TTM)	2.49
52 Week High	39.00	P/E (TTM)	52.30
52 Week Low	6.88	Price/Book (MRQ)	8.24
Beta	-0.16	Price/Cash Flow (TTM)	50.96
Avg Daily Vol (10 Day)	0.04 Mil	ROA (TTM)	10.08%
Avg Daily Vol (3 Month)	0.01 Mil	ROE (TTM)	19.37%
		Current Ratio (MRQ)	1.78
DIVIDEND INFORMATION		Total Debt/Equity (MRQ)	0.06
Indicated Annual ($)	0.00		
Yield	0.00%		

NOTE: TTM = trailing twelve months
MRQ = most recent quarter

SHARE RELATED INFORMATION		SHORT INTEREST INFORMATION	
Market Cap. ($)	1,456.704 Mil	Current Month	0.040 Mil
Shares Out.	40.605 Mil	Previous Month	0.044 Mil
Float	30.000 Mil	Short Interest Ratio	5.0 Day

INSTITUTIONAL & INSIDER OWNERSHIP

	PURCHASES	SALES	NET PURCH	%OWNED
Institutions (3 Months)	0.308 Mil	0.009 Mil	0.299 Mil	2.3%
Insiders (6 Months)	0.000 Mil	0.000 Mil	0.000 Mil	26.1%

BUSINESS SUMMARY
Logitech International SA is engaged in the design,
manufacture and marketing of a variety of computer interface
devices, including input and pointing devices such as mice,
trackballs and keyboards, as well as joysticks, gamepads and
imaging devices. For the FY ended 3/31/00, net sales rose
31% to $615.7M. Net income totaled $30M, up from $7.1M.
Results reflect increased sales of keyboards, mice and PC
video cameras and the absence of product line sale losses.

REVENUES (Thousands of U.S. Dollars)

QUARTERS	1997	1998	1999	2000
JUN	84,362	90,158	73,015	121,067
SEP	92,248	99,159	95,816	133,247
DEC	128,757	114,826	154,506	185,425
MAR	108,349	86,084	147,404	175,925
TOTAL	413,716	390,227	470,741	615,664

EARNINGS PER SHARE

	1997	1998	1999	2000
JUN	0.690	0.550	0.130	0.145
SEP	0.970	0.920	-1.840	1.265
DEC	3.125	2.290	2.425	3.430
MAR	1.755	0.145	1.020	2.020
TOTAL	6.540	3.905	1.735	6.860

All financials are reported according to U.S. GAAP.

GROWTH RATES	1 YEAR	3 YEAR	5 YEAR
Revenue	30.79%	14.17%	15.25%
EPS	283.37%	3.57%	28.77%
Dividend	NM%	NM%	-100.00%

(Load Date: 7/17/00)
Database: Quick Facts
Keyword(s): (LOGIY)

End of Report

CHART B-12

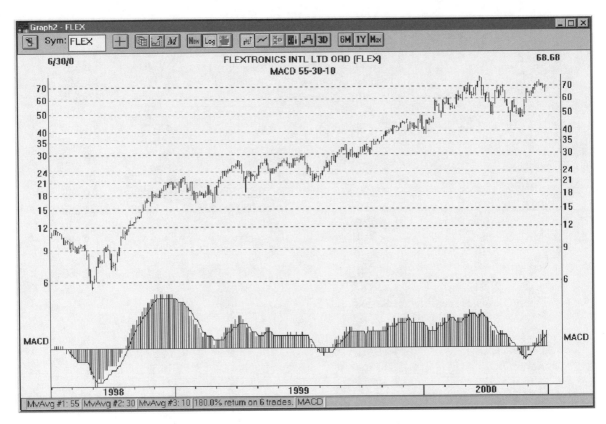

Courtesy of Telescan, Inc.

Flextronics International, LTD. current 2 year

Quick Facts
QKFACT FLEX   Y2573F102 Flextronics International

Market Guide Quick Facts Report

Flextronics International	SYMBOL: FLEX	EXCHANGE:	NASD

PRICING DATA (AS OF)	07/14/00	RATIOS & STATISTICS	
Price	83.75	Price/Revenue (TTM)	2.31
52 Week High	84.81	P/E (TTM)	83.17
52 Week Low	21.25	Price/Book (MRQ)	6.61
Beta	2.60	Price/Cash Flow (TTM)	77.98
Avg Daily Vol (10 Day)	2.50 Mil	ROA (TTM)	6.41%
Avg Daily Vol (3 Month)	3.35 Mil	ROE (TTM)	14.39%
		Current Ratio (MRQ)	1.83
DIVIDEND INFORMATION		Total Debt/Equity (MRQ)	0.31
Indicated Annual ($)	NM		
Yield	NA%	NOTE: TTM = trailing twelve months	
		MRQ = most recent quarter	

SHARE RELATED INFORMATION		SHORT INTEREST INFORMATION	
Market Cap. ($)	16,226.395 Mil	Current Month	2.842 Mil
Shares Out.	193.748 Mil	Previous Month	2.020 Mil
Float	127.900 Mil	Short Interest Ratio	0.8 Day

INSTITUTIONAL & INSIDER OWNERSHIP

	PURCHASES	SALES	NET PURCH	%OWNED
Institutions (3 Months)	30.291 Mil	9.818 Mil	20.472 Mil	59.8%
Insiders (6 Months)	0.000 Mil	0.703 Mil	-0.703 Mil	34.0%

BUSINESS SUMMARY
Flextronics International provides electronics
manufacturing services to OEMs in the networking, computer,
medical, consumer and telecommunications industries. For
the FY ended 3/31/00, net sales rose 93% to $4.31B. Net
income rose 99% to $120.9M. Revenues reflect the Company's
ability to expand sales to new customers worldwide and
increased sales at existing customers. Earnings also
reflect a reduction in unusual charges.

REVENUES (Thousands of U.S. Dollars)

QUARTERS	1997	1998	1999	2000
JUN	149,782	235,545	427,501	685,641
SEP	156,757	251,468	515,394	941,760
DEC	161,248	295,000	631,932	1,251,681
MAR	172,220	331,058	658,381	1,428,111
TOTAL	640,007	1,113,071	2,233,208	4,307,193

EARNINGS PER SHARE

	1997	1998	1999	2000
JUN	0.075	0.095	0.140	0.170
SEP	0.085	0.090	0.170	0.250
DEC	-0.003	0.075	0.180	0.310
MAR	0.013	0.010	0.140	0.270
TOTAL	0.170	0.270	0.630	1.000

FY'98-'99 and FY'99-'00 Q's are restated for poolings with
PCB Assembly and Kyrel EMS.4/3/00, Company acquired The
Dii Group for 62,768,139 shares (pooling of interests).

GROWTH RATES	1 YEAR	3 YEAR	5 YEAR
Revenue	92.87%	88.80%	71.28%
EPS	63.00%	82.55%	52.97%
Dividend	NM%	NM%	NM%

(Load Date: 7/17/00)
Database: Quick Facts
Keyword(s): (FLEX)

End of Report

CHART B-13

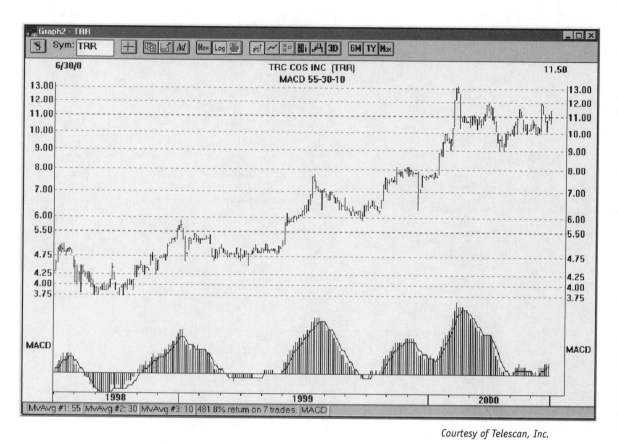

Courtesy of Telescan, Inc.

TRC Companies, Inc. current 2 year

Quick Facts
QKFACT TRR   872625108 TRC Companies, Inc.

Market Guide Quick Facts Report

TRC Companies, Inc.	SYMBOL: TRR	EXCHANGE:	NYSE

PRICING DATA (AS OF)	07/14/00	RATIOS & STATISTICS	
Price	10.88	Price/Revenue (TTM)	1.02
52 Week High	13.25	P/E (TTM)	19.18
52 Week Low	5.94	Price/Book (MRQ)	1.48
Beta	0.61	Price/Cash Flow (TTM)	11.50
Avg Daily Vol (10 Day)	0.01 Mil	ROA (TTM)	5.91%
Avg Daily Vol (3 Month)	0.01 Mil	ROE (TTM)	8.33%
		Current Ratio (MRQ)	1.70
DIVIDEND INFORMATION		Total Debt/Equity (MRQ)	0.26
Indicated Annual ($)	0.00		
Yield	0.00%	NOTE: TTM = trailing twelve months	
		MRQ = most recent quarter	

SHARE RELATED INFORMATION		SHORT INTEREST INFORMATION	
Market Cap. ($)	74.798 Mil	Current Month	0.006 Mil
Shares Out.	6.878 Mil	Previous Month	0.000 Mil
Float	3.000 Mil	Short Interest Ratio	0.4 Day

INSTITUTIONAL & INSIDER OWNERSHIP

	PURCHASES	SALES	NET PURCH	%OWNED
Institutions (3 Months)	0.014 Mil	0.045 Mil	-0.031 Mil	26.9%
Insiders (6 Months)	0.002 Mil	0.014 Mil	-0.013 Mil	56.4%

BUSINESS SUMMARY
TRC Companies, together with its subsidiaries,
provide technical, financial risk management & construction
services to industry and government in U.S. markets. For
the 9 months ended 3/00, revenues rose 45% to $58.2M. Net
income rose 96% to $3.2M. Results reflect continued
internal growth and additional revenue from acquisitions.
Net income benefited from an improved gross profit margin
and lower operating expenses as a percentage of revenues.

REVENUES (Thousands of U.S. Dollars)

QUARTERS	1997	1998	1999	2000
SEP	13,385	12,990	12,880	18,113
DEC	12,725	12,944	13,151	18,754
MAR	11,868	12,919	14,071	21,326
JUN	12,810	13,856	17,231	
TOTAL	50,788	52,709	57,333	

EARNINGS PER SHARE

	1997	1998	1999	2000
SEP	0.020	0.020	0.070	0.130
DEC	0.030	0.040	0.080	0.150
MAR	-0.090	0.040	0.090	0.170
JUN	-0.030	0.060	0.120	
TOTAL	-0.070	0.160	0.360	

FY'97 B/S are reclassified.FY'92 & FY'93 annual and FY'94 Q. fncls. are restated due to the pooling of interest acquisition of Mariah Associates, Inc.

GROWTH RATES	1 YEAR	3 YEAR	5 YEAR
Revenue	8.77%	-1.51%	-1.23%
EPS	126.58%	NM%	2.53%
Dividend	NM%	NM%	NM%

(Load Date: 7/17/00)
Database: Quick Facts
Keyword(s): (TRR)

End of Report

CHART B-14

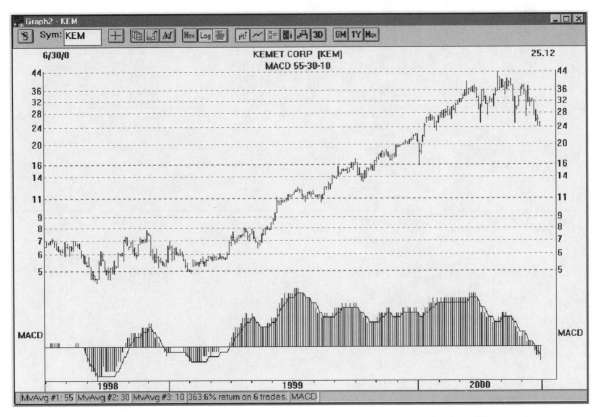

Courtesy of Telescan, Inc.

Kemet Corporation current 2 year

Quick Facts
QKFACT KEM   488360108 KEMET Corporation

Market Guide Quick Facts Report

KEMET Corporation	SYMBOL: KEM	EXCHANGE:	NYSE

PRICING DATA (AS OF)	07/14/00	RATIOS & STATISTICS	
Price	29.00	Price/Revenue (TTM)	2.86
52 Week High	44.22	P/E (TTM)	33.76
52 Week Low	10.56	Price/Book (MRQ)	4.61
Beta	0.80	Price/Cash Flow (TTM)	18.67
Avg Daily Vol (10 Day)	2.65 Mil	ROA (TTM)	9.61%
Avg Daily Vol (3 Month)	1.56 Mil	ROE (TTM)	18.75%
		Current Ratio (MRQ)	2.38
DIVIDEND INFORMATION		Total Debt/Equity (MRQ)	0.18
Indicated Annual ($)	0.00		
Yield	0.00%	NOTE: TTM = trailing twelve months	
		MRQ = most recent quarter	

SHARE RELATED INFORMATION		SHORT INTEREST INFORMATION	
Market Cap. ($)	2,534.890 Mil	Current Month	2.140 Mil
Shares Out.	87.410 Mil	Previous Month	1.276 Mil
Float	62.100 Mil	Short Interest Ratio	1.9 Day

INSTITUTIONAL & INSIDER OWNERSHIP

	PURCHASES	SALES	NET PURCH	%OWNED
Institutions (3 Months)	25.876 Mil	16.081 Mil	9.795 Mil	90.1%
Insiders (6 Months)	0.001 Mil	3.041 Mil	-3.040 Mil	29.0%

BUSINESS SUMMARY
KEM and subsidiaries are engaged in the manufacture
and sale of solid tantalum and multilayer ceramic capacitors
in the worldwide market under the KEMET brand name. For the
FY ended 3/31/00, revenues rose 45% to $822.1M. Net income
totalled $70.1M, up from $6.2M. Revenues benefitted from
higher demand for surface-mount tantalum and multi-layer
ceramic capacitors. Earnings benefitted from Company's
cost reduction activities and higher margins.

REVENUES (Thousands of U.S. Dollars)

QUARTERS	1997	1998	1999	2000
JUN	125,726	161,204	142,471	162,649
SEP	130,192	165,477	137,733	186,187
DEC	143,626	170,359	141,914	215,139
MAR	155,775	170,681	143,451	258,120
TOTAL	555,319	667,721	565,569	822,095

EARNINGS PER SHARE

	1997	1998	1999	2000
JUN	0.125	0.180	0.020	0.060
SEP	0.005	0.180	0.005	0.110
DEC	0.155	0.095	0.025	0.220
MAR	0.190	0.170	0.030	0.460
TOTAL	0.475	0.625	0.080	0.850

12/99, Exchange changed from NASDAQ. FY'93 Q. EPS reflects increased shs o/s due to 10/92 IPO.

GROWTH RATES	1 YEAR	3 YEAR	5 YEAR
Revenue	45.36%	13.97%	11.68%
EPS	991.03%	21.63%	16.24%
Dividend	NM%	NM%	NM%

(Load Date: 7/17/00)
Database: Quick Facts
Keyword(s): (KEM)

End of Report

CHART B-15

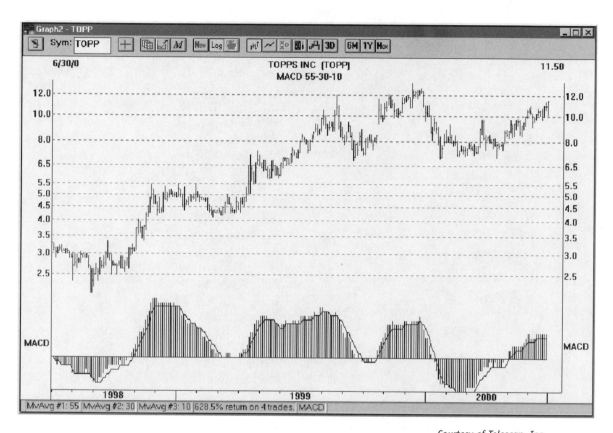

Topps Company, Inc current 2 year

Quick Facts
QKFACT TOPP   890786106 The Topps Company, Inc. UPDATED

Market Guide Quick Facts Report

The Topps Company, Inc.	SYMBOL: TOPP	EXCHANGE:	NASD

PRICING DATA (AS OF)	07/14/00	RATIOS & STATISTICS	
Price	11.50	Price/Revenue (TTM)	1.26
52 Week High	13.38	P/E (TTM)	6.89
52 Week Low	6.81	Price/Book (MRQ)	3.41
Beta	0.99	Price/Cash Flow (TTM)	6.58
Avg Daily Vol (10 Day)	0.64 Mil	ROA (TTM)	38.10%
Avg Daily Vol (3 Month)	0.52 Mil	ROE (TTM)	67.72%
		Current Ratio (MRQ)	2.19
DIVIDEND INFORMATION		Total Debt/Equity (MRQ)	0.00
Indicated Annual ($)	0.00		
Yield	0.00%	NOTE: TTM = trailing twelve months	
		MRQ = most recent quarter	

SHARE RELATED INFORMATION		SHORT INTEREST INFORMATION	
Market Cap. ($)	522.790 Mil	Current Month	0.203 Mil
Shares Out.	45.460 Mil	Previous Month	0.196 Mil
Float	39.100 Mil	Short Interest Ratio	0.5 Day

INSTITUTIONAL & INSIDER OWNERSHIP

	PURCHASES	SALES	NET PURCH	%OWNED
Institutions (3 Months)	4.544 Mil	7.474 Mil	-2.930 Mil	38.5%
Insiders (6 Months)	0.070 Mil	0.010 Mil	0.060 Mil	14.0%

BUSINESS SUMMARY
TOPP is marketer of collectible picture products.
TOPP also distributes Bazooka brand bubble gum, novelty
candy products, branded lollipops, collectible toys, comic
books, and sticker and album collections. For the 13 weeks
ended 5/27/00, net sales rose 70% to $144.3M. Net income
rose from $9.3M to $29M. Revenues reflect increased sales
of confectionery and entertainment products. Earnings also
reflect favorable product mix and reduction in loan balance.

REVENUES (Thousands of U.S. Dollars)

QUARTERS	1998	1999	2000	2001
MAY	60,177	53,327	84,941	144,332
AUG	55,118	57,868	80,391	
NOV	54,173	67,647	110,777	
FEB	71,782	50,572	98,084	
TOTAL	241,250	229,414	374,193	

EARNINGS PER SHARE

	1998	1999	2000	2001
MAY	0.020	0.060	0.200	0.620
AUG	-0.040	0.100	0.210	
NOV	-0.180	0.090	0.460	
FEB	0.110	0.080	0.380	
TOTAL	-0.090	0.330	1.250	

FY'92 & FY'91 financials and FY'93 Q's are reclassified.
FY'95 - '96 financials are reclassified.

GROWTH RATES	1 YEAR	3 YEAR	5 YEAR
Revenue	63.11%	11.63%	7.11%
EPS	273.65%	NM%	30.09%
Dividend	NM%	NM%	-100.00%

(Load Date: 7/17/00)
Database: Quick Facts
Keyword(s): (TOPP)

End of Report

CHART B-16

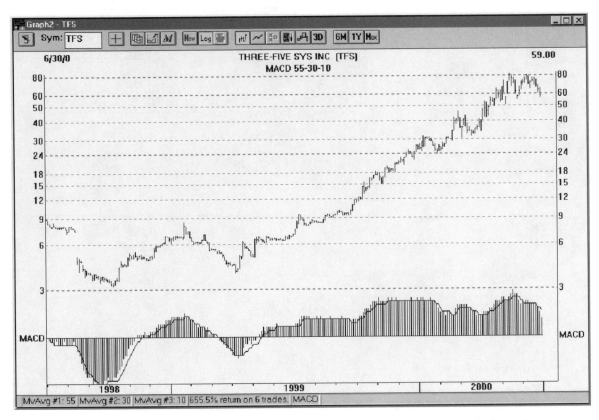

Courtesy of Telescan, Inc.

Three-Five Systems current 2 year

Quick Facts
QKFACT TFS   88554L108 Three-Five Systems, Inc. UPDATED

Market Guide Quick Facts Report

Three-Five Systems, Inc.   SYMBOL: TFS   EXCHANGE: NYSE

PRICING DATA (AS OF)	07/14/00	RATIOS & STATISTICS	
Price	35.00	Price/Revenue (TTM)	3.70*
52 Week High	82.50	P/E (TTM)	45.99*
52 Week Low	8.03	Price/Book (MRQ)	6.29
Beta	1.38	Price/Cash Flow (TTM)	34.35
Avg Daily Vol (10 Day)	1.44 Mil	ROA (TTM)	12.11%*
Avg Daily Vol (3 Month)	0.63 Mil	ROE (TTM)	16.60%*
		Current Ratio (MRQ)	4.24
DIVIDEND INFORMATION		Total Debt/Equity (MRQ)	0.00
Indicated Annual ($)	0.00		
Yield	0.00%	NOTE: TTM = trailing twelve months	
		MRQ = most recent quarter	

SHARE RELATED INFORMATION		SHORT INTEREST INFORMATION	
Market Cap. ($)	664.720 Mil	Current Month	0.727 Mil
Shares Out.	18.992 Mil	Previous Month	0.222 Mil
Float	17.400 Mil	Short Interest Ratio	1.2 Day

INSTITUTIONAL & INSIDER OWNERSHIP

	PURCHASES	SALES	NET PURCH	%OWNED
Institutions (3 Months)	NM Mil	NM Mil	NM Mil	NM%
Insiders (6 Months)	0.000 Mil	0.006 Mil	-0.006 Mil	8.4%

BUSINESS SUMMARY
TFS designs and manufactures a wide range of display
modules for use in the end products of original equipment
manufacturers. The Co. specializes in liquid crystal display
components and technology. For the three months ended 3/00,
sales rose 70% to $39.2M. Net income totaled $3.6M vs.a
loss of $642K. Revenues reflect increased worldwide demand
for mobile handsets. Net income reflects higher margins,
lower S/G/A and R & D expenses as a percentage of sales.

PRELIMINARY: For the 3 months ended 06/30/2000, revenues
were 44,926; after tax earnings were 4,369. (expressed in Thousands

REVENUES (Thousands of U.S. Dollars)

QUARTERS	1997	1998	1999	2000
MAR	16,129	18,479	23,044	39,162
JUN	18,737	22,682	31,600	44,926*
SEP	24,074	24,572	42,723	
DEC	25,702	29,314	50,041	
TOTAL	84,642	95,047	147,408	

EARNINGS PER SHARE

	1997	1998	1999	2000
MAR	0.050	0.060	-0.047	0.180
JUN	0.065	0.070	0.073	0.210*
SEP	0.095	-0.025	0.140	
DEC	0.115	0.060	0.233	
TOTAL	0.325	0.165	0.399	

FY'94 Q. financials are reclassified.FY'97 & '98 Q's are reclassified.1/95, Company began trading on NYSE.

GROWTH RATES	1 YEAR	3 YEAR	5 YEAR
Revenue	55.09%	34.40%	11.52%
EPS	160.84%	NM%	-11.44%
Dividend	NM%	NM%	NM%

(Load Date: 7/17/00)
Database: Quick Facts
Keyword(s): (TFS)

End of Report

CHART B-17

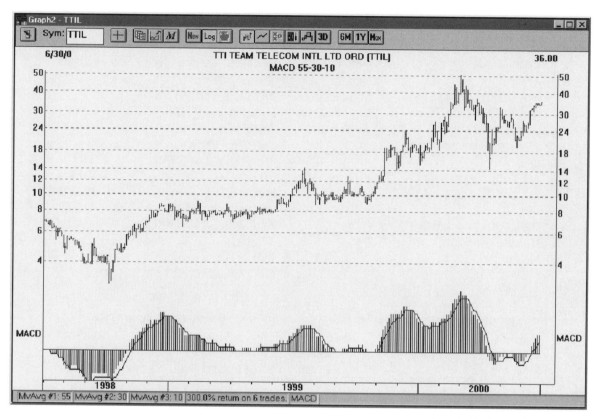

Courtesy of Telescan, Inc.

TTI Telecom International, LTD current 2 year

Quick Facts
QKFACT TTIL   M88258104 TTI Team Telecom Intl.

Market Guide Quick Facts Report

TTI Team Telecom Intl.	SYMBOL: TTIL	EXCHANGE:	NASD

PRICING DATA (AS OF)	07/14/00	RATIOS & STATISTICS	
Price	36.00	Price/Revenue (TTM)	11.25
52 Week High	51.13	P/E (TTM)	62.07
52 Week Low	8.75	Price/Book (MRQ)	9.86
Beta	1.31	Price/Cash Flow (TTM)	62.07
Avg Daily Vol (10 Day)	0.07 Mil	ROA (TTM)	13.69%
Avg Daily Vol (3 Month)	0.10 Mil	ROE (TTM)	18.22%
		Current Ratio (MRQ)	3.82
DIVIDEND INFORMATION		Total Debt/Equity (MRQ)	0.00
Indicated Annual ($)	0.00		
Yield	0.00%	NOTE: TTM = trailing twelve months	
		MRQ = most recent quarter	

SHARE RELATED INFORMATION		SHORT INTEREST INFORMATION	
Market Cap. ($)	345.600 Mil	Current Month	0.006 Mil
Shares Out.	9.600 Mil	Previous Month	0.005 Mil
Float	4.300 Mil	Short Interest Ratio	0.1 Day

INSTITUTIONAL & INSIDER OWNERSHIP

	PURCHASES	SALES	NET PURCH	%OWNED
Institutions (3 Months)	2.050 Mil	0.326 Mil	1.724 Mil	36.7%
Insiders (6 Months)	0.000 Mil	0.000 Mil	0.000 Mil	55.2%

BUSINESS SUMMARY
TTI Telecom International designs, develops, markets
and supports advanced, modular, integrated software products
and provides services for network management and operations
support in the telecommunications industry. For the 3
months ended 3/00, total revenues increased 53% to $9.7M.
Net income increased 44% to $1.7M. Revenues reflect higher
product sales. Net income was partially offset by increased
research and development expenses.

REVENUES (Thousands of U.S. Dollars)

QUARTERS	1997	1998	1999	2000
MAR	2,652	4,011	6,361	9,709
JUN	2,842	4,369	7,221	
SEP	3,150	4,974	8,028	
DEC	3,542	5,747	9,251	
TOTAL	12,186	19,101	30,861	

EARNINGS PER SHARE

	1997	1998	1999	2000
MAR	0.050	0.070	0.130	0.160
JUN	0.060	0.070	0.130	
SEP	0.060	0.090	0.140	
DEC	0.080	0.130	0.160	
TOTAL	0.250	0.360	0.560	

3/99, 12/99 & 3/00 Cash Flows are N/A.12/99 Q = 9 months.

GROWTH RATES	1 YEAR	3 YEAR	5 YEAR
Revenue	61.57%	58.13%	NM%
EPS	55.50%	77.04%	NM%
Dividend	NM%	NM%	NM%

(Load Date: 7/17/00)
Database: Quick Facts
Keyword(s): (TTIL)

End of Report

CHART B-18

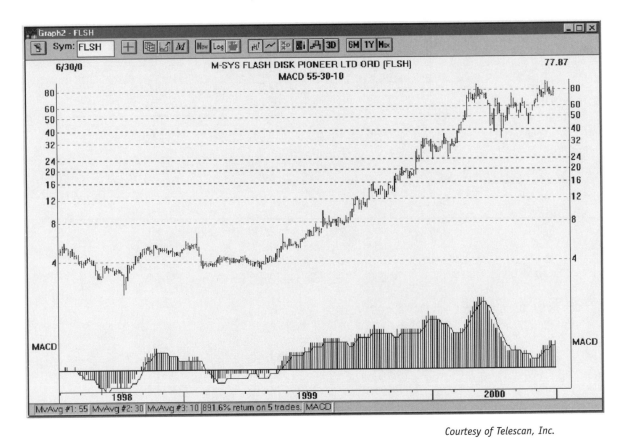

Courtesy of Telescan, Inc.

M-Systems Inc. current 2 year

Quick Facts
QKFACT FLSH   M7061C100 M-Systems Inc.

Market Guide Quick Facts Report

M-Systems Inc.	SYMBOL: FLSH	EXCHANGE:	NASD

PRICING DATA (AS OF)	07/14/00	RATIOS & STATISTICS	
Price	82.00	Price/Revenue (TTM)	NA*
52 Week High	93.72	P/E (TTM)	NA*
52 Week Low	6.38	Price/Book (MRQ)	49.44
Beta	0.62	Price/Cash Flow (TTM)	NM
Avg Daily Vol (10 Day)	0.40 Mil	ROA (TTM)	NA%*
Avg Daily Vol (3 Month)	0.35 Mil	ROE (TTM)	6.36%*
		Current Ratio (MRQ)	2.90
DIVIDEND INFORMATION		Total Debt/Equity (MRQ)	0.00
Indicated Annual ($)	0.00		
Yield	0.00%	NOTE: TTM = trailing twelve months	
		MRQ = most recent quarter	

SHARE RELATED INFORMATION		SHORT INTEREST INFORMATION	
Market Cap. ($)	863.870 Mil	Current Month	0.062 Mil
Shares Out.	10.535 Mil	Previous Month	0.027 Mil
Float	8.200 Mil	Short Interest Ratio	0.2 Day

INSTITUTIONAL & INSIDER OWNERSHIP

	PURCHASES	SALES	NET PURCH	%OWNED
Institutions (3 Months)	3.107 Mil	0.334 Mil	2.774 Mil	42.3%
Insiders (6 Months)	0.000 Mil	0.000 Mil	0.000 Mil	22.2%

BUSINESS SUMMARY
FLSH develops, manufactures and sells electronic
disks that provide data storage based on flash memory for
embedded systems, telecommunication applications & internet
appliances. For the FY ended 12/31/99, revenues rose 86% to
$30.4M. Net loss totalled $1.7M, up from $270K. Revenues
reflect the penetration of Co.'s existing products into new
markets, and the release of the new DiskOnChip Millenium.
Net loss reflects increased selling and marketing expenses.

PRELIMINARY: For the 3months ended 03/31/2000, revenues
were 15,204; after tax earnings were 1,112. (expressed in Thousands)

REVENUES (Thousands of U.S. Dollars)

QUARTERS	1997	1998	1999	2000
MAR	3,827	0	0	15,204*
JUN	4,560	7,732	11,275	
SEP	4,767	3,758	8,070	
DEC	5,880	4,861	11,085	
TOTAL	19,034	16,351	30,430	

EARNINGS PER SHARE

	1997	1998	1999	2000
MAR	-0.480	0.000	0.000	0.090*
JUN	-0.040	0.080	-0.140	
SEP	-0.040	-0.020	-0.030	
DEC	0.010	-0.080	0.000	
TOTAL	-0.550	-0.020	-0.170	

1/95 private placement of 484,373 units (2 Common + 1
Warrant) @ $7.68.Quarterly C/F are NA.

GROWTH RATES	1 YEAR	3 YEAR	5 YEAR
Revenue	86.11%	37.33%	44.77%
EPS	NM%	NM%	NM%
Dividend	NM%	NM%	NM%

(Load Date: 7/17/00)
Database: Quick Facts
Keyword(s): (FLSH)

End of Report

CHART B-19

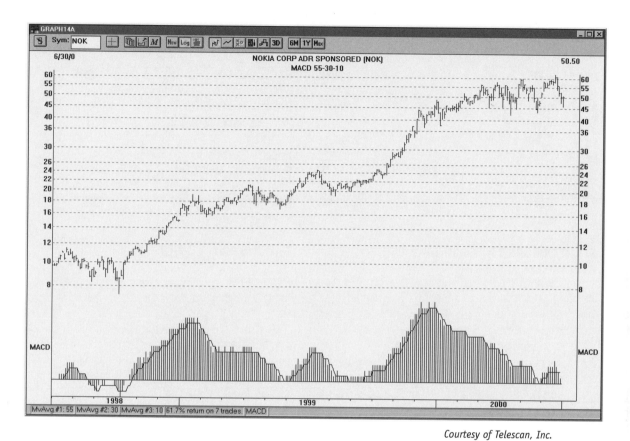

Courtesy of Telescan, Inc.

Nokia Corporation current 2 year

Quick Facts
QKFACT NOK   654902204 Nokia Corporation

Market Guide Quick Facts Report

Nokia Corporation	SYMBOL: NOK	EXCHANGE:	NYSE

PRICING DATA (AS OF)	07/14/00	RATIOS & STATISTICS	
Price	55.00	Price/Revenue (TTM)	12.36*
52 Week High	62.50	P/E (TTM)	93.54*
52 Week Low	19.27	Price/Book (MRQ)	36.98
Beta	1.92	Price/Cash Flow (TTM)	102.04
Avg Daily Vol (10 Day)	10.68 Mil	ROA (TTM)	24.78%*
Avg Daily Vol (3 Month)	11.39 Mil	ROE (TTM)	48.36%*
		Current Ratio (MRQ)	1.69

DIVIDEND INFORMATION		Total Debt/Equity (MRQ)	0.14
Indicated Annual ($)	0.77		
Yield	1.39%	NOTE: TTM = trailing twelve months	
		MRQ = most recent quarter	

SHARE RELATED INFORMATION		SHORT INTEREST INFORMATION	
Market Cap. ($)	255973.300 Mil	Current Month	6.672 Mil
Shares Out.	4,654.060 Mil	Previous Month	6.558 Mil
Float	4,607.500 Mil	Short Interest Ratio	0.7 Day

INSTITUTIONAL & INSIDER OWNERSHIP

	PURCHASES	SALES	NET PURCH	%OWNED
Institutions (3 Months)	163.590 Mil	88.820 Mil	74.770 Mil	28.2%
Insiders	(6 Months)	0.000 Mil	0.000 Mil	0.000 Mil
1.0%				

BUSINESS SUMMARY
Nokia is a supplier of telecommunications systems &
equipment. The Company's core businesses include the
development, manufacture and delivery of operator-driven
infrastructure solutions and end-user-driven mobile phones.
For the FY ended 12/31/99, sales rose 48% to EUR19.77B. Net
income according to U.S. GAAP before accounting change rose
51% to EUR2.54B. Results reflect strong demand for the
Company's mobile phone products and higher gross margins.

PRELIMINARY: For the 3months ended 03/31/2000, revenues
were 6,537; after tax earnings were 891. (expressed in Millions)

ADR INFORMATION
Shares Per ADR   1.000
Most Recent Currency Rate   1.066

REVENUES (Millions of Euro)

QUARTERS	1997	1998	1999	2000
MAR	1,906	2,501	3,870	6,537*
JUN	2,197	3,098	4,493	
SEP	2,079	3,375	5,037	
DEC	2,667	4,352	6,372	
TOTAL	8,849	13,326	19,772	

EARNINGS PER SHARE

	1997	1998	1999	2000
MAR	0.040	0.058	0.108	0.190*
JUN	0.049	0.078	0.123	
SEP	0.057	0.099	0.135	
DEC	0.057	0.123	0.175	
TOTAL	0.203	0.358	0.541	

4/99, Co. combined Common Class A and K to form a new class
of Common Stock. Qrtly. results do not reflect U.S. GAAP.
Summ Q's Translated from FMA to EUR @ 5.94573 FMA-1 EUR.

GROWTH RATES	1 YEAR	3 YEAR	5 YEAR
Revenue	48.37%	44.06%	31.26%
EPS	48.92%	67.53%	34.01%
Dividend	54.84%	48.29%	35.47%

(Load Date: 7/17/00)
Database: Quick Facts
Keyword(s): (NOK)

End of Report

CHART B-20

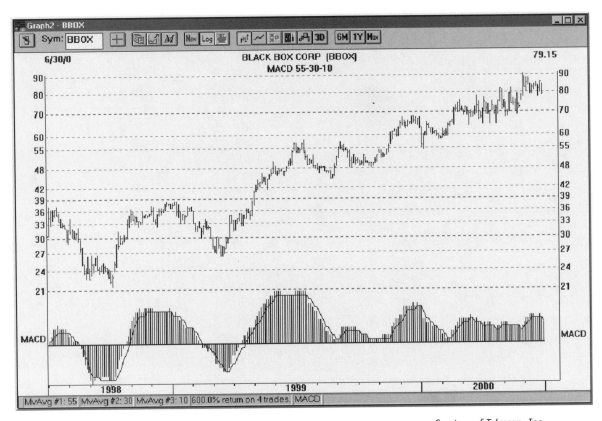

Courtesy of Telescan, Inc.

Black Box Corporation current 2 year

Quick Facts
QKFACT BBOX   091826107 Black Box Corporation   UPDATED

Market Guide Quick Facts Report

Black Box Corporation	SYMBOL: BBOX	EXCHANGE:	NASD

PRICING DATA (AS OF)	07/14/00	RATIOS & STATISTICS	
Price	61.19	Price/Revenue (TTM)	2.05*
52 Week High	92.25	P/E (TTM)	22.39*
52 Week Low	44.56	Price/Book (MRQ)	4.37
Beta	0.95	Price/Cash Flow (TTM)	19.24
Avg Daily Vol (10 Day)	0.70 Mil	ROA (TTM)	15.33%*
Avg Daily Vol (3 Month)	0.26 Mil	ROE (TTM)	25.54%*
		Current Ratio (MRQ)	2.48
DIVIDEND INFORMATION		Total Debt/Equity (MRQ)	0.41
Indicated Annual ($)	0.00		
Yield	0.00%	NOTE: TTM = trailing twelve months	
		MRQ = most recent quarter	

SHARE RELATED INFORMATION		SHORT INTEREST INFORMATION	
Market Cap. ($)	1,146.724 Mil	Current Month	0.300 Mil
Shares Out.	18.741 Mil	Previous Month	0.249 Mil
Float	11.100 Mil	Short Interest Ratio	1.5 Day

INSTITUTIONAL & INSIDER OWNERSHIP

	PURCHASES	SALES	NET PURCH	%OWNED
Institutions (3 Months)	2.364 Mil	2.286 Mil	0.078 Mil	84.1%
Insiders (6 Months)	0.001 Mil	0.018 Mil	-0.017 Mil	40.8%

BUSINESS SUMMARY
BBOX is a direct marketer and technical service
provider of computer communications and networking equipment
and services to businesses of all sizes, operating in 77
countries. For the FY ended 3/31/00, revenues increased 51%
to $499.8M. Net income increased 28% to $48.9M. Revenues
reflect the Company's continued expansion of its technical
services capabilities. Net income was partially offset by a
decreased gross profit margin.

PRELIMINARY: For the 3 months ended 06/30/2000, revenues
were 169,036; after tax earnings were 14,128. (expressed in Thousands)

REVENUES (Thousands of U.S. Dollars)

QUARTERS	1998	1999	2000	2001
JUN	69,269	73,096	97,520	169,036*
SEP	74,596	79,130	117,889	
DEC	74,206	84,789	127,128	
MAR	81,205	92,959	157,279	
TOTAL	299,276	329,974	499,816	

EARNINGS PER SHARE

	1998	1999	2000	2001
JUN	0.400	0.460	0.570	0.720*
SEP	0.440	0.490	0.620	
DEC	0.450	0.530	0.650	
MAR	0.510	0.620	0.750	
TOTAL	1.800	2.100	2.590	

8/94, Co. changed name from MB Communications to Black Box
Corp.FY'97 - '99 fncls. are restated due to the
acquisition of 5 businesses.

GROWTH RATES	1 YEAR	3 YEAR	5 YEAR
Revenue	51.47%	26.59%	24.85%
EPS	24.57%	23.05%	24.03%
Dividend	NM%	NM%	NM%

(Load Date: 7/17/00)
Database: Quick Facts
Keyword(s): (BBOX)

End of Report

Samples of Prior MAGNET® Stocks

Chart C-1

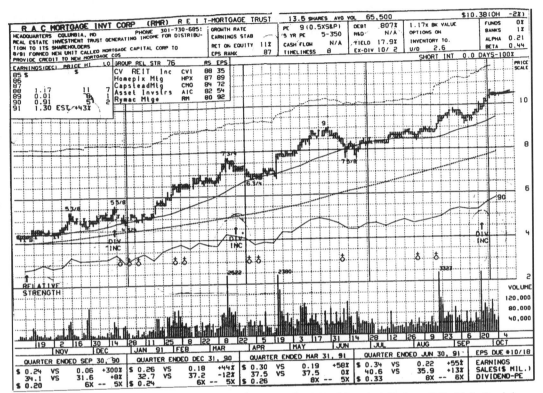

Courtesy of Investor's Business Daily (Daily Graphs)

RAC MORTGAGE (name changed to DYNEX CAPITAL)

M: Unusually strong insider buying, great steady momentum.

A: Accelerating margins resulting from loans with greater profits.

G: Trading at six times expected earnings-great discount to growth rate.

N: New business plan was transforming company into high growth.

E: Emerging and creative mortgage programs are dramatically improving margins.

T: Technically in a powerful uptrend with higher bottoms and tops.

NOTE: This stock was paying almost an 18% cash dividend at the time!

Chart C-2

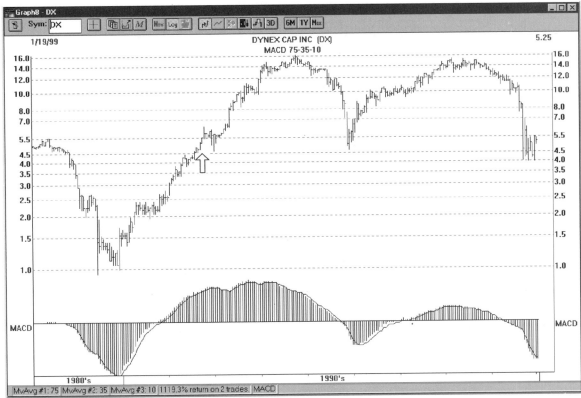

Courtesy of Telescan, Inc.

DYNEX CAPITAL (formerly RAC MORTGAGE)

When I found this stock in 1991 it looked too good to be true. Tremendous insider buying, along with three dividend increases within one year made this even more "Magnetic". We received another opportunity on this stock again (See Chapter 9).

Chart C-3

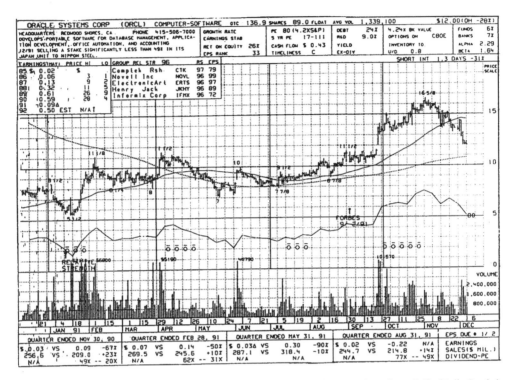

Courtesy of Investor's Business Daily (Daily Graphs)

ORACLE

M: Hard-driving management owned about 40% of outstanding shares

A: Earnings and revenues were starting to show renewed growth following write-offs and charges from prior year.

G: It was impossible at the time to realize how inexpensive this stock really was due to prior losses, and to assign a valuation.

N: New networking capabilities were making Oracle's database product immensely attractive in what would later be called the technical revolution.

E: Database management was an emerging industry and Oracle continued to develop and progress through new products and upgrades.

T: Stock had six months of improving relative strength following a dramatic selloff. It broke out of a long base on heavy volume, and pulled back on light volume to create an excellent entry point.

Chart C-4

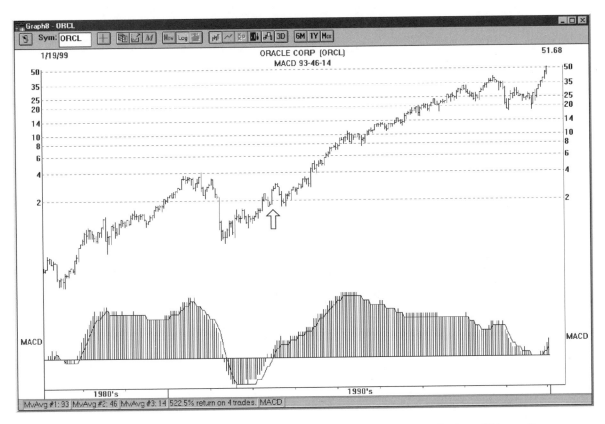

Courtesy of Telescan, Inc.

ORACLE

This company was one of my first big winners, and it helped teach me many lessons. It took time for Oracle to really regain its uptrend, and this taught me about patience in investing. Once the stock got moving, I sold too early, and I learned another lesson about how powerful a MAGNET® stock can be if given the requisite amount of time!

Chart C-5

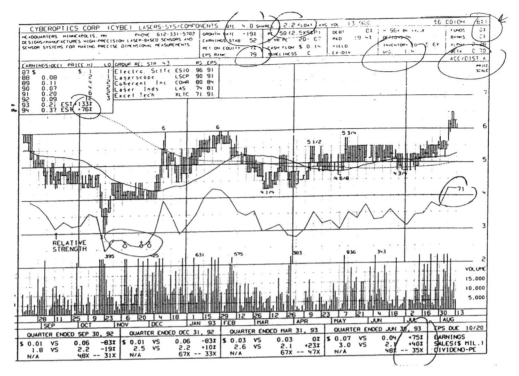

Courtesy of Investor's Business Daily (Daily Graphs)

CYBEROPTICS

M: Management owned almost 40% of outstanding shares.

A: Revenues, margins and earnings started to explode.

G: The expected p/e of 35 looked high but not relative to the expected growth rate.

N: New measuring technology had multiple applications in various industries.

E: Laser measurement represented an emerging industry.

T: Technically trying to break out of base, still early-the perfect time to accumulate a stock.

Chart C-6

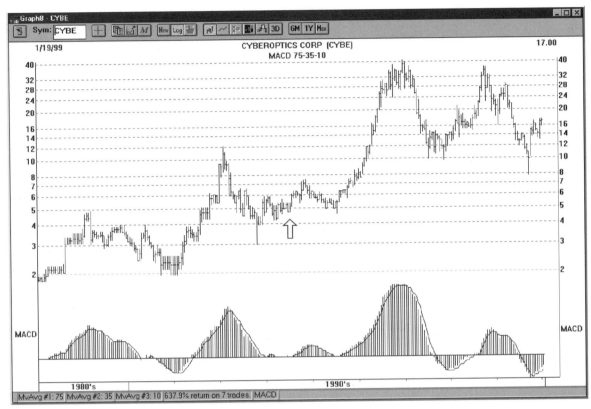

Courtesy of Telescan, Inc.

CYBEROPTICS

I bought Cyberoptics when there was no institutional ownership. As a result, I was early-waiting almost a full year before the stock moved. In this case, the wait was worth it! Again, I sold too soon, but remember, MAGNET® stocks often lose their "pull" and do not always remain market favorites.

Chart C-7

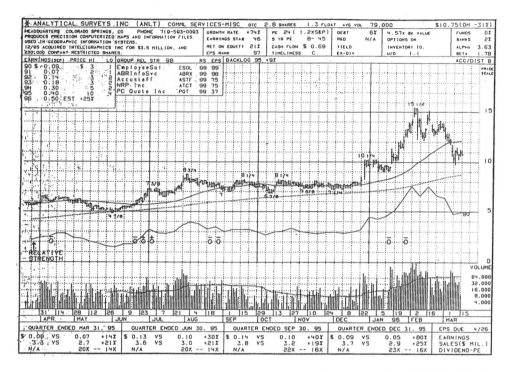

Courtesy of Investor's Business Daily (Daily Graphs)

ANALYTICAL SURVEYS

M: Strong management team owned more than half the outanding shares.

A: Earnings, revenues and margins all showed powerful acceleration.

G: Stock was trading at ¹/₄ of its expected growth rate and ¹/₂ of it's estimated next years earning growth, providing a significant discount.

N: New technology in precision mapping had various new applications.

E: Innovative management developed even further uses of their technology in emerging applications and industries.

T: Powerful uptrend was beginning following a two-year base. Excellent pullback entry point was provided when the company's stock returned to the prior breakout point near $11.00 per share.

Chart C-8

Courtesy of Telescan, Inc.

ANALYTICAL SURVEYS

Although Analytical Surveys had no institutional following at this time, a powerful uptrend was beginning and within a short period its MAGNET® attraction brought in many top momentum money managers.

Chart C-9

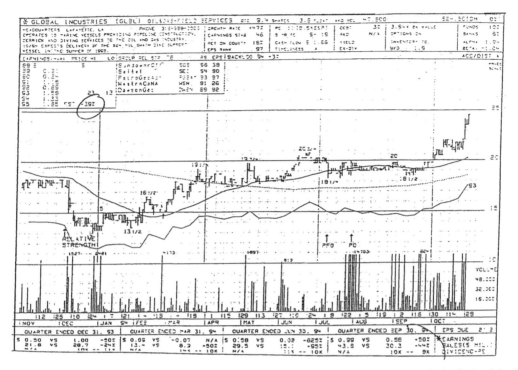

Courtesy of Investor's Business Daily (Daily Graphs)

GLOBAL INDUSTRIES

M: Management owned more than 50% of outstanding shares.

A: Earnings, revenues and margins showed dramatic acceleration.

G: The expected price earnings ratio of only 8 offered great discount to growth rate.

N: New efforts in drilling off Gulf of Mexico would be a catalyst for many oil drillers at this time.

E: Emerging technology in deep water drilling was dramatically improving margins.

T: Stock was emerging from a long base with a surge in volume. The relative strength was showing months of improvement and the moving average was beginning to go higher.

Chart C-10

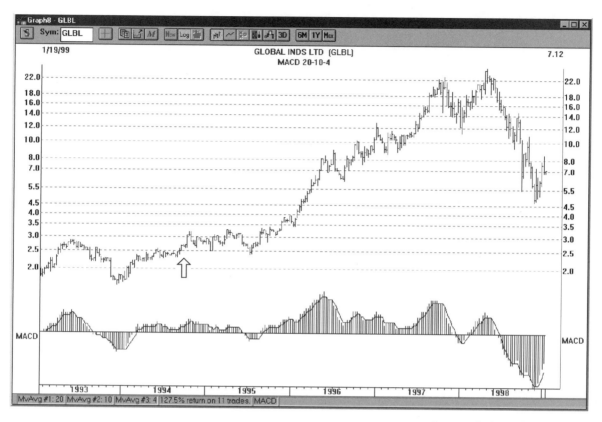

Courtesy of Telescan, Inc.

GLOBAL INDUSTRIES

Global Industries stock showed dramatic returns as it was discovered by institutions and the group became strong. This particular company was one of the first in the group to show increasing relative strength. Global Industries went on to be a true market leader. Once again, as the group fell apart, so did this company's stock price. Negative sector forces can drain the "Magnetic" pull out of most stocks.

Chart C-11

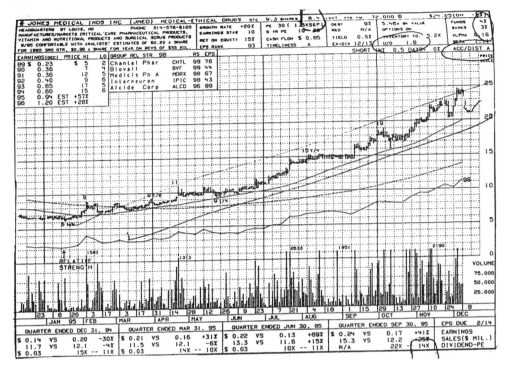

Courtesy of Investor's Business Daily (Daily Graphs)

JONES MEDICAL

(subsequent name change to Jones Pharmaceutical Inc.)

M: Management owned about 30% of outstanding shares.

A: Earnings, revenues and margins were all improving.

G: The low P/E of 14 was largely discounted to the projected 50+% increase in earnings

N: New products were driving margins higher

E: Emerging trends in healthcare were benefiting company

T: Stock was in a powerful and steady uptrend.

Chart C-12

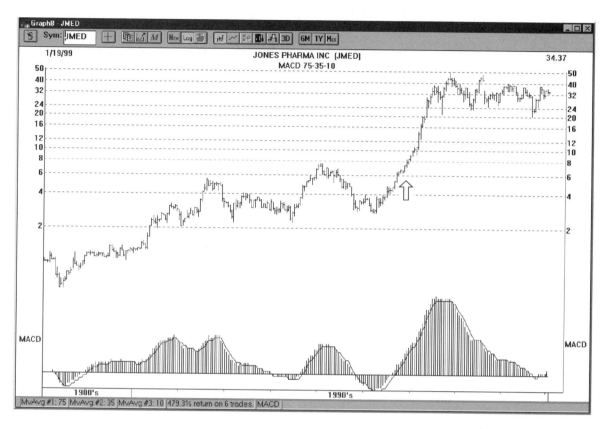

Courtesy of Telescan, Inc.

Jones Medical

I did not invest in this company in 1995 because, looking at the chart, I thought I was too late. This serves as a reminder—do not underestimate a company's ability to continue to grow or what the market will pay for a growth stock.

Chart C-13

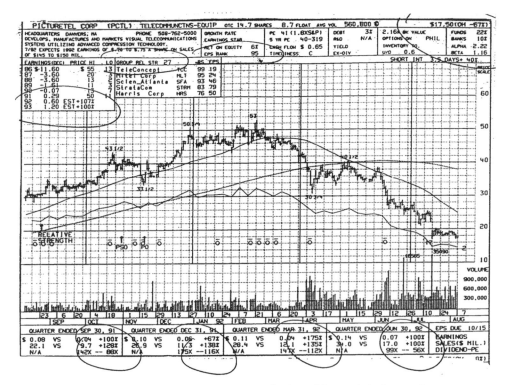

Courtesy of Investor's Business Daily (Daily Graphs)

PICTURETEL CORP.

M: Management owned over 35% of outstanding shares.

A: Strong earnings and revenue growth.

G: Stock was trading at 50% of expected growth.

N: Video conferencing was a brand new technology.

E: Emerging new industry was dazzling Wall Street.

T: Stock was in a downtrend with no signs of a bottom

Chart C-14

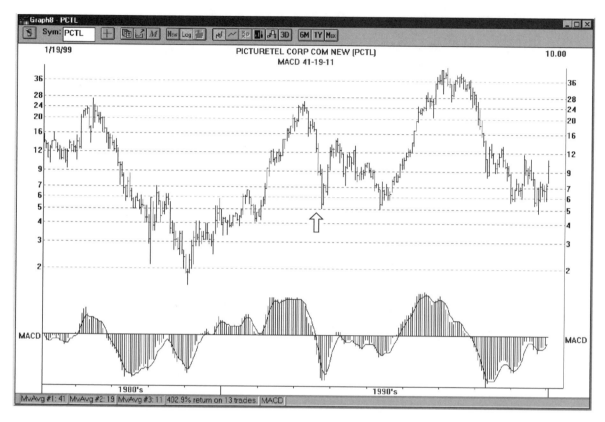

Courtesy of Telescan, Inc.

PICTURETEL CORP.

Great events were taking place at the company and I uncharacteristically bought right at the bottom. The stock jumped over six times in value before starting to decline again.

Chart C-15

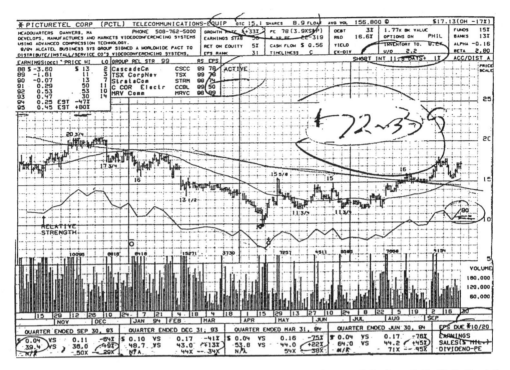

Courtesy of Investor's Business Daily (Daily Graphs)

PICTURETEL CORP.

(revisited)

M: Management owned about 50% of outstanding shares.

A: Revenues were accelerating once again, along with the company's story.

G: The P/E was high but the stock was still trading at a discount to the expected growth rate.

N: Picturetel was leading the industry in advances in video conferencing.

E: This emerging industry was attracting investor attention.

T: Stock began showing positive relative strength following a two-year sell-off.

Chart C-16

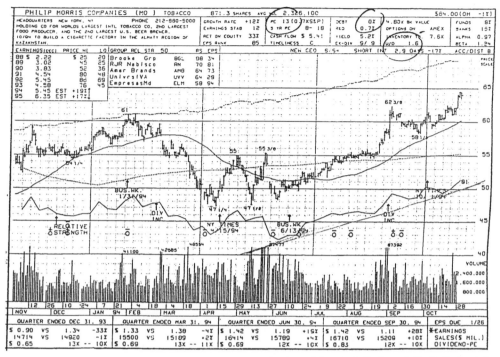

Courtesy of Investor's Business Daily (Daily Graphs)

PHILIP MORRIS

M: Management structure and personnel known for superior results.

A: Acceleration of revenues, margins and earnings following prior year dip.

G: With a 10 P/E, Philip Morris was trading at a 50% discount to its growth rate.

N: Company was expanding its dominant brands into new overseas markets.

E: Emerging markets were opening overseas, leading to further expansion.

T: Stock was showing six months of positive relative strength while still being down 20% off its previous high three years earlier. This represented another great entry point into one of the best all time investments.

Chart C-17

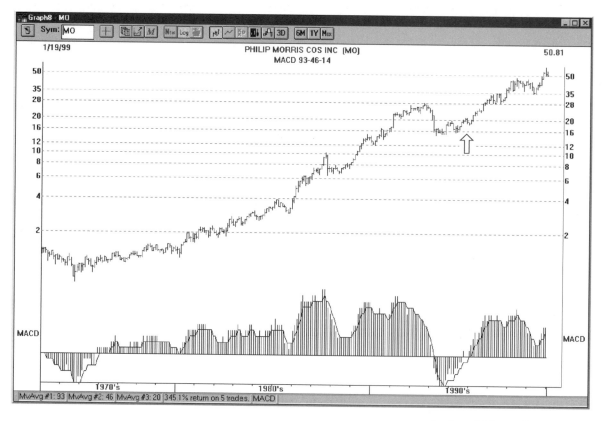

Courtesy of Telescan, Inc.

PHILIP MORRIS

This Dow stock doubled within two years after reestablishing momentum. If you had bought this stock at the 1993 bottom, you would have tripled your money, but I preferred to wait for a new uptrend.

Chart C-18

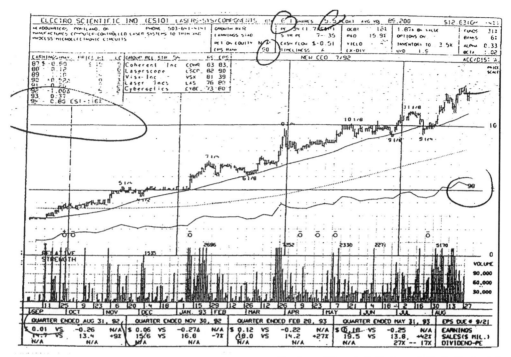

Courtesy of Investor's Business Daily (Daily Graphs)

ELECTRO SCIENTIFIC INDUSTRIES

M: A new CEO had been named.

A: Revenues, earnings margins all powerfully accelerating.

G: A P/E of 17 made this company a good value based on growth rate.

N: New products brought company into industry focus.

E: Emerging new industry was dazzling Wall Street.

T: Stock was in a technically powerful and steady uptrend.

Chart C-19

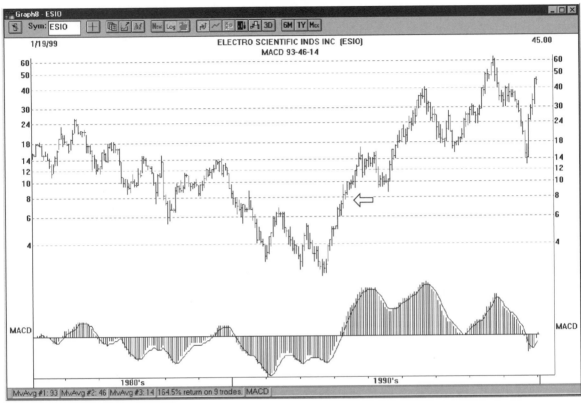

Courtesy of Telescan, Inc.

ELECTRO SCIENTIFIC INDUSTRIES

I found this stock while studying the sector. I owned Cyberoptics and saw some strength emerging in the group. Group strength and sector rotation can be very important.

GLOSSARY

Accrued Interest: Coupon interest accumulated on a bond or note since the last interest payment or, for a new issue, from the dated date (original date of issue) to the date of delivery.

Asset Allocation. Distributing investment funds among various assets, such as cash, stock, fixed-income investments, and tangible assets (real estate, precious metals, and collectibles).

Basis Point: One one-hundredth of one percent.

Benchmark Bonds. A bond whose price and yield will be representative of an entire section of the market.

Blue Sky Law: A legal term referring to various state laws enacted to protect the public against securities fraud. These laws describe the method and form of registration of municipal bonds in each particular state.

Breakout. A price movement beyond a previous high (or low) or outside the boundaries of a preceding price consolidation.

Certificate of Deposit (CD). A time deposit with a specified maturity date.

Chart Analysis. The study of price charts in an effort to find patterns that, in the past, preceded price advances or declines.

Compounding. The process by which interest is paid on interest that has been previously earned.

Contrarian Investing. The contrarian philosophy is to buy when everyone else is selling and vice versa. The rationale is that when everyone is bearish, a market must go up because there are no sellers left; conversely, when everyone is bullish, a market must go down because there are no buyers left.

Convertible Bond. A bond that may be exchanged for common stock.

Credit Risk. This is primarily associated with investments in bonds. It involves the possibility that the issuer of a fixed income security will default and be unable to pay the principal and interest stated in the original terms of the bond.

Current Yield. Annual income divided by the price of the security, i.e. annual return.

Current Yield (Bonds): The ratio of the coupon rate on a bond to the dollar purchase price, expressed as a percentage.

Dated Date: The date carried on the face of a bond or note from which interest normally begins to accrue.

Debt Ratio. The ratio of debt to total assets; a measure of the use of debt financing.

Default: The failure to pay principal and/or interest when due, or a breach of the agreement.

Discount Rate. The rate of interest charged by the Federal Reserve when banks borrow reserves from the Fed.

Double Barreled Bond: A bond with two distinct pledged sources of revenue such as earmarked moneys from a specific source or aid payments, as well as the general obligation taxing powers of the issuer.

Dow Theory. Some analysts believe that similar direction and change in both the Industrial Average and the Transportation Average will confirm a major stock market trend. Both averages have to make new highs or new lows to confirm a trend.

Earnings Per Share (EPS). The net income of a company divided by the average number of shares outstanding during the period.

Equivalent Taxable Yield. This compares the nontaxable yield on a municipal bond to the taxable yield on a corporate bond at a specified investors tax bracket.

Fixed-Income Investment. A debt security that pays a fixed rate of return and guarantees repayment of principal at a specified maturity date. Examples of fixed-income investments include government, corporate, or municipal bonds; also equity securities such as a preferred stock, which will not always have a specified maturity, but whose dividend and principal is protected ahead of the company's common shareholders.

Fundamental Analysis. The analysis of a company and industry and economic data to forecast the business prospects of the company.

Good Delivery: The physical delivery of bonds upon sale, which fulfills all legal requirements necessary for the change of ownership.

Growth Stock. The shares of a company whose earnings are expected to grow at an above average rate from one business cycle to the next.

Inflation. An economic condition of price increases occurring when the demand for goods and services outstrips the economy's ability to produce them.

Inflation Risk. This is the risk associated with earning a positive rate of return on your investments but still eroding your purchasing power. The rate of return on investment assets must be greater than inflation. Inflation risk is much less discussed but has severe consequences to many fixed income investors.

Interest Rate Risk. Rising interest rates will usually cause market values to decline; thereby causing fixed income securities and some equities to lose their value.

Liquidity Risk. Sometimes an asset cannot be converted to cash when needed. This is more common in investments other than registered securities.

Long-term Debt. Corporate debt that comes due after more than one year.

magnet® Stock. Contains a combination of technical and fundamental characteristics that pull investors into the shares, resulting in a rapid price increase.

Market Risk. The uncertainty of how the market will value an investment asset at any given point in time. This is the kind of risk most people think about. Market risk includes fluctuation and volatility of prices, and the possibility of losing the full investment (i.e. there is no longer a market for the security you purchased).

Momentum Investing. An investment approach that involves locating companies whose sales, earnings growth, or price are increasing at a significantly faster rate than the market as a whole. This discipline is less concerned with price to earnings, price to sales, or other traditional methods of valuation in favor of more rapid price appreciation.

Momentum/Growth Stock. A "high flying" stock that is expected to continue growing at a fast rate. These stocks typically trade at a high price/earnings ratio.

Moving Average. An average in which the most recent observation is added and the most distant observation is deleted before the average is recomputed. Fifty-day and two hundred day moving averages are commonly used by investors while traders use shorter periods.

Municipal Bond. A tax-exempt bond; a bond issued by a state or one of its political subdivisions.

Negotiated Sale: The sale of a bond issue where an underwriter(s) negotiates the terms and conditions of the sale with the bond buyers, on behalf of an issuer.

Original Issue Discount: A bond issued at an offering price substantially below par; the appreciation from the original price to par over the life of the bonds is treated as tax-exempt income.

Overbought/Oversold Indicator. A technical indicator that attempts to define when prices have risen (declined) too far and/or too fast, and hence are vulnerable to a reaction in the opposite direction.

Point and Figure Chart. A charting technique that plots the price movements of a stock to identify the market forces of supply and demand. The charts move in intervals so that minor price fluctuations do not obscure the true price trend.

Price Earnings Ratio (PE). The price of a stock divided by its earnings per share.

Price to Call: The yield of a bond priced to the first call date rather than to maturity.

Principal. The dollar amount of an investment at the point of purchase.

Refunding Bond: The issuance of a new bond for the purpose of retiring an already outstanding bond issue.

Reinvestment Risk. This risk is associated with fixed income securities. It considers the possibility that maturing investments will be reinvested at lower rates of return. Those owning bonds or bank deposits that paid high rates of interest in the early 1980's became painfully aware of this risk in recent years.

Relative Strength. In the stock market, a measure of a given stock's price strength relative to a broad index of stocks. The term can also be used in a more general sense to refer to an overbought/oversold type of indicator.

Relative Earnings Strength. This compares a company's earnings growth against the market as a whole.

Sector Rotation. A top down investment approach that identifies a group of stocks across several industries that will benefit from changes in the business cycle.

Sentiment Indicator. A measure of the balance between bullish and bearish opinions. Contrarian investors often uses sentiment indicators. The put/call option ratio is one example of a sentiment indicator.

Sinking Fund: Money set aside on a periodic basis to retire term bonds at or prior to maturity.

Stochastics. A technical indicator that measures the position of a stock (or option) in comparison to its most recent trading range to indicate over-bought and oversold conditions.

Taxable Equivalent Yield: The yield an investor would have to obtain on a taxable corporate or U.S. government bond to match the same after tax yield on a municipal bond.

Tax Risk. This occurs when a change in the tax laws reduces the market value of an investment. For example, real estate investments were hurt badly in the 1980's when the tax laws were changed. The municipal bond market continues to be threatened by changes in the tax code that would affect their tax-exempt status, although this is unlikely to occur.

Technical Analysis. An analysis of a stock's price and volume behavior used to forecast future price performance.

Trading Flat: Bonds that trade at their principal amount with no accrued interest included, usually in default.

Treasury Notes. The intermediate-term debt of the federal government.

Value Investing. A long-term investment approach that attempts to identify undervalued stocks, according to their price and projected future earnings. Companies that trade at a low price to sales, price to earnings, or price to growth rate will be identified using value investing.

Volume Analysis. A technical tool used to anticipate a significant move in a stock price and confirm a change in trend. An increase in the daily trading volume of a stock is often a forerunner to a significant price move. An increase in trading volume after a significant price move helps to confirm a change in trend.

Yield Curve. The relationship between time to maturity and yields for debt in a given risk class.

Yield to Call. The yield earned on a bond from the time it is acquired until the time it is called and retired by the issuer.

Yield to Maturity. The percentage rate of return paid on a bond if you buy and hold it to its maturity date. The calculation is based on the coupon rate, length of time to maturity, and market price. It assumes that coupon interest paid over the life of the bond will be reinvested at the same rate.

Zero Coupon Bonds: Zero coupons bonds allow investors to compound their principal over time, but pay no cash dividends. The current value of these bonds is quite volatile and often misunderstood by investors.

Index

**USE THIS FORM IF THIS BOOK IS NOT
AVAILABLE AT YOUR LOCAL BOOKSTORE**

Order Form

SHIP TO:

YOUR NAME AND TITLE:_____

NAME OF ORGANIZATION:_____

STREET ADDRESS:_____

CITY:_____ STATE:_____ ZIP:_____

TELEPHONE:_____

FAX:_____

E-MAIL:_____

Please send the following:

_____Copies of MAGNET® INVESTING (2nd Edition)
at $24.95 per book

Shipping: $4.00 for first book, $1.00 for each additional book.
New Jersey residents add 6% sales tax.

A check for $_____ is enclosed.

Orders must be prepaid unless using an official purchase order.

Mail to:

Next Decade, Inc.
39 Old Farmstead Road
Chester, NJ 07930
Telephone (908) 879-6625 / Fax: (908) 879-2920
e-mail: barbara@nextdecade.com / www.nextdecade.com